BATTLES FOR ATLANTA

Sherman Moves East

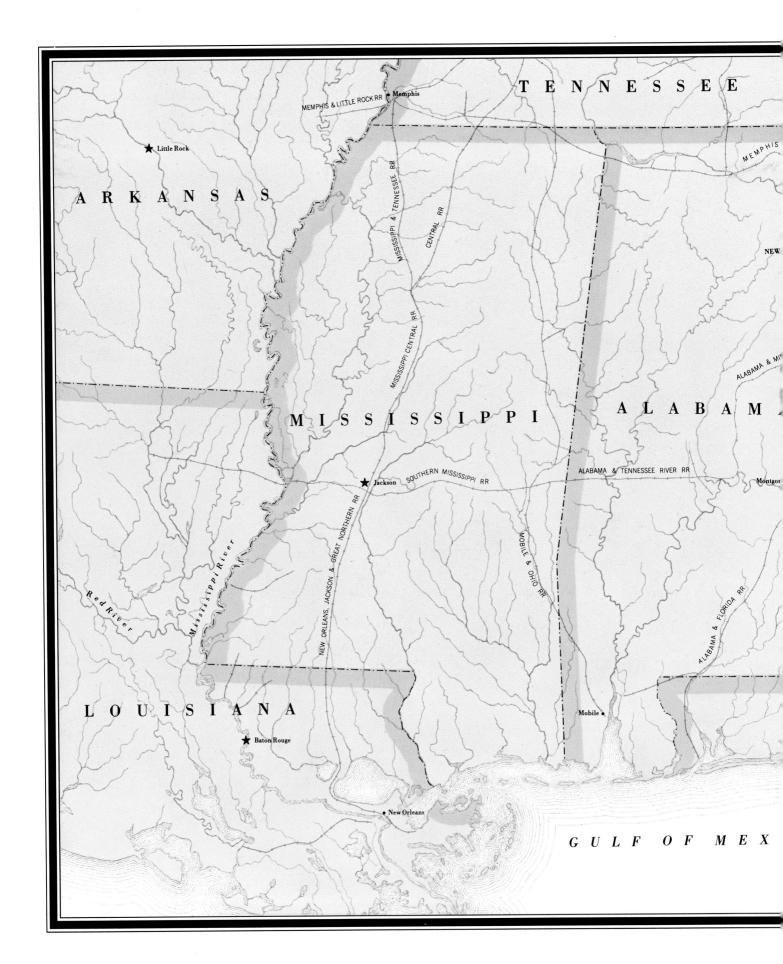

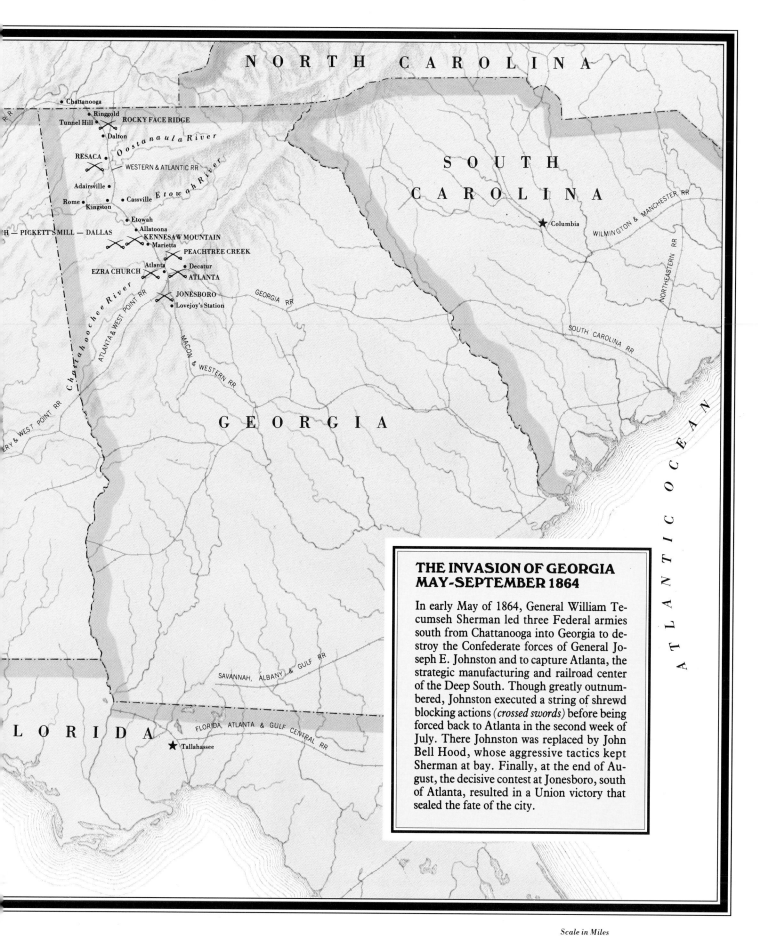

NORTH CAROLINA

Chattanooga
Ringgold
ROCKY FACE RIDGE
Tunnel Hill
Dalton
Oostanaula River
RESACA
WESTERN & ATLANTIC RR
Etowah River
Adairsville
Rome
Kingston
Cassville
Etowah
H — PICKETT'S MILL — DALLAS
Allatoona
KENNESAW MOUNTAIN
Marietta
PEACHTREE CREEK
Atlanta
Decatur
EZRA CHURCH
ATLANTA
Chattahoochee River
JONESBORO
Lovejoy's Station
ATLANTA & WEST POINT RR
GEORGIA RR
MACON & WESTERN RR
GEORGIA
ERY & WEST POINT RR

SOUTH CAROLINA
Columbia
WILMINGTON & MANCHESTER RR
NORTHEASTERN RR
SOUTH CAROLINA RR

ATLANTIC OCEAN

SAVANNAH, ALBANY & GULF RR
LORIDA
FLORIDA, ATLANTA & GULF CENTRAL RR
Tallahassee

THE INVASION OF GEORGIA
MAY–SEPTEMBER 1864

In early May of 1864, General William Tecumseh Sherman led three Federal armies south from Chattanooga into Georgia to destroy the Confederate forces of General Joseph E. Johnston and to capture Atlanta, the strategic manufacturing and railroad center of the Deep South. Though greatly outnumbered, Johnston executed a string of shrewd blocking actions (*crossed swords*) before being forced back to Atlanta in the second week of July. There Johnston was replaced by John Bell Hood, whose aggressive tactics kept Sherman at bay. Finally, at the end of August, the decisive contest at Jonesboro, south of Atlanta, resulted in a Union victory that sealed the fate of the city.

Scale in Miles

0   25   50   100   150

TIME® LIFE BOOKS

Other Publications:

THE NEW FACE OF WAR
HOW THINGS WORK
WINGS OF WAR
CREATIVE EVERYDAY COOKING
COLLECTOR'S LIBRARY OF THE UNKNOWN
CLASSICS OF WORLD WAR II
TIME-LIFE LIBRARY OF CURIOUS AND UNUSUAL FACTS
AMERICAN COUNTRY
VOYAGE THROUGH THE UNIVERSE
THE THIRD REICH
THE TIME-LIFE GARDENER'S GUIDE
MYSTERIES OF THE UNKNOWN
TIME FRAME
FIX IT YOURSELF
FITNESS, HEALTH & NUTRITION
SUCCESSFUL PARENTING
HEALTHY HOME COOKING
UNDERSTANDING COMPUTERS
LIBRARY OF NATIONS
THE ENCHANTED WORLD
THE KODAK LIBRARY OF CREATIVE PHOTOGRAPHY
GREAT MEALS IN MINUTES
PLANET EARTH
COLLECTOR'S LIBRARY OF THE CIVIL WAR
THE EPIC OF FLIGHT
THE GOOD COOK
WORLD WAR II
HOME REPAIR AND IMPROVEMENT
THE OLD WEST

This volume is one of a series that chronicles in full
the events of the American Civil War, 1861-1865.
Other books in the series include:
Brother against Brother: The War Begins
First Blood: Fort Sumter to Bull Run
The Blockade: Runners and Raiders
The Road to Shiloh: Early Battles in the West
Forward to Richmond: McClellan's Peninsular Campaign
Decoying the Yanks: Jackson's Valley Campaign
Confederate Ordeal: The Southern Home Front
Lee Takes Command: From Seven Days to Second Bull Run
The Coastal War: Chesapeake Bay to Rio Grande
Tenting Tonight: The Soldier's Life
The Bloodiest Day: The Battle of Antietam
War on the Mississippi: Grant's Vicksburg Campaign
Rebels Resurgent: Fredericksburg to Chancellorsville
Twenty Million Yankees: The Northern Home Front
Gettysburg: The Confederate High Tide
The Struggle for Tennessee: Tupelo to Stones River
The Fight for Chattanooga: Chickamauga to Missionary Ridge
Spies, Scouts and Raiders: Irregular Operations
The Killing Ground: Wilderness to Cold Harbor
Sherman's March: Atlanta to the Sea
Death in the Trenches: Grant at Petersburg
War on the Frontier: The Trans-Mississippi West
The Shenandoah in Flames: The Valley Campaign of 1864
Pursuit to Appomattox: The Last Battles
The Assassination: The Death of the President
The Nation Reunited: War's Aftermath
Master Index: An Illustrated Guide

The Cover: General William Tecumseh Sherman (*center, on horseback*), accompanied by an officer using field glasses, consults the commander of an artillery battery during a bombardment of Atlanta. Behind them, General William F. Barry, Sherman's artillery chief, sees to the disposition of his forces.

For information on and a full description of any of the
Time-Life Books series listed on this page, please call
1-800-621-7026 or write:
Reader Information
Time-Life Customer Service
P.O. Box C-32068
Richmond, Virginia 23261-2068

THE CIVIL WAR

BATTLES FOR ATLANTA

BY

RONALD H. BAILEY

AND THE

EDITORS OF TIME-LIFE BOOKS

Sherman Moves East

TIME-LIFE BOOKS, ALEXANDRIA, VIRGINIA

Time-Life Books is a division of Time Life Inc.,
a wholly owned subsidiary of
THE TIME INC. BOOK COMPANY

TIME-LIFE BOOKS

PRESIDENT: Mary N. Davis

Managing Editor: Thomas H. Flaherty
Director of Editorial Resources: Elise D. Ritter-Clough
Director of Photography and Research:
John Conrad Weiser
Editorial Board: Dale M. Brown, Roberta Conlan,
Laura Foreman, Lee Hassig, Jim Hicks, Blaine
Marshall, Rita Thievon Mullin, Henry Woodhead

PUBLISHER: Robert H. Smith

Associate Publisher: Trevor Lunn
Editorial Director: Donia Steele
Marketing Director: Regina Hall
Production Manager: Marlene Zack
Supervisor of Quality Control: James King

Editorial Operations
Production: Celia Beattie
Library: Louise D. Forstall
Computer Composition: Deborah G. Tait (Manager),
Monika D. Thayer, Janet Barnes Syring, Lillian
Daniels

The Civil War
Series Director: Henry Woodhead
Designer: Edward Frank
Series Administrator: Philip Brandt George

Editorial Staff for *Battles for Atlanta*
Associate Editors: Susan V. Kelly, Jeremy Ross (pictures)
Staff Writers: Thomas H. Flaherty Jr., Stephen G.
Hyslop, Daniel Stashower, David S. Thomson
Researchers: Harris J. Andrews, Kristin Baker
(principals); Stephanie Lewis, Mark Moss,
Brian C. Pohanka
Assistant Designer: Cynthia T. Richardson
Copy Coordinator: Jayne E. Rohrich
Picture Coordinator: Betty H. Weatherley
Editorial Assistant: Donna Fountain
Special Contributor: Brian McGinn

Editorial Operations
Copy Chief: Diane Ullius
Editorial Operations: Caroline A. Boubin (manager)
Production: Celia Beattie
Quality Control: James J. Cox (director)
Library: Louise D. Forstall

Correspondents: Elisabeth Kraemer-Singh (Bonn);
Margot Hapgood, Dorothy Bacon (London); Miriam
Hsia (New York); Maria Vincenza Aloisi, Josephine du
Brusle (Paris); Ann Natanson (Rome). Valuable
assistance was also provided by: Carolyn Chubet
(New York).

The Author:
Ronald H. Bailey is a freelance journalist and author who
has written on a variety of subjects for Time-Life Books.
He is the author of *Violence and Aggression* in the Human
Behavior series, several volumes in the World War II series, *Glacier* in the Planet Earth series, *Forward to Richmond* and *The Bloodiest Day* in the Civil War series.

The Consultants:
Colonel John R. Elting, USA (Ret.), a former Associate
Professor at West Point, is the author of *Battles for Scandi-
navia* in the Time-Life Books World War II series and of
*The Battle of Bunker's Hill, The Battles of Saratoga, Mili-
tary History and Atlas of the Napoleonic Wars, American
Army Life* and *The Superstrategists.* Co-author of *A
Dictionary of Soldier Talk,* he is also editor of the three
volumes of *Military Uniforms in America, 1755-1867,* and
associate editor of *The West Point Atlas of American Wars.*

William A. Frassanito, a Civil War historian and lecturer
specializing in photograph analysis, is the author of two
award-winning studies, *Gettysburg: A Journey in Time* and
*Antietam: The Photographic Legacy of America's Bloodiest
Day,* and a companion volume, *Grant and Lee, The Virginia Campaigns.* He has also served as chief consultant to the
photographic history series *The Image of War.*

Les Jensen, Director of the Second Armored Division
Museum, Fort Hood, Texas, specializes in Civil War arti-
facts and is a conservator of historic flags. He is a contributor to *The Image of War* series, a consultant for numerous
Civil War publications and museums, and a member of
the Company of Military Historians. He was formerly Curator of the U.S. Army Transportation Museum at Fort
Eustis, Virginia, and before that Curator of the Museum
of the Confederacy in Richmond, Virginia.

Michael McAfee specializes in military uniforms and has
been Curator of Uniforms and History at the West Point
Museum since 1970. A fellow of the Company of Military
Historians, he coedited with Colonel Elting *Long Endure:
The Civil War Years,* and he collaborated with Frederick
Todd on *American Military Equipage.* He is the author of
Artillery of the American Revolution, 1775-1783, and has
written numerous articles for *Military Images Magazine.*

James P. Shenton, Professor of History at Columbia University, is a specialist in 19th-century American political
and social history, with particular emphasis on the Civil
War period. He is the author of *Robert John Walker* and
Reconstruction South.

Library of Congress Cataloguing in Publication Data
Bailey, Ronald H.
  The battles for Atlanta.
  (The Civil War)
  Bibliography: p.
  Includes index.
  1. Atlanta Campaign, 1864.   I. Time-Life Books.
II. Title.   III. Series.
E476.7.B26 1986   973.7'37   85-24521
ISBN 0-8094-4773-8
ISBN 0-8094-4772-X (lib. bdg.)

CONTENTS

The Hard Road
to Atlanta

Bristling with confidence, Major General William Tecumseh Sherman led his Federal army into Georgia in May of 1864 on a crucial mission — to seize the city of Atlanta in the heart of the Deep South.

Between Sherman's main base at Chattanooga and his objective loomed two daunting obstacles. One was General Joseph E. Johnston's Confederate Army of Tennessee — outnumbered but defending home ground. The other was 120 miles of wild land that until a generation earlier had been the domain of Cherokee Indians.

George Barnard, a civilian photographer who accompanied Sherman's army, later compiled a graphic record of this terrain, as shown on these pages. The direct path for the Federals lay southeast down the route of the Western & Atlantic Railroad. Steep gorges and raging rivers sliced across the path, and thick forests cut visibility to 100 yards or less. Rutted wagon tracks led to rickety bridges that could easily be destroyed. In all, it was ideal country for a fighting retreat, and Johnston made the most of his advantage, bloodying Sherman's nose at every turn. After a month, however, the Federals had slogged across 100 miles of Georgia — until Atlanta lay just over the horizon.

A vital trestle bridge linking the
Union base at Chattanooga with supply sources farther north is defended by log blockhouses at either end
and by a permanent garrison of
troops housed in tents. "Every foot of
the way," wrote General Sherman,
"had to be strongly guarded against
the acts of a local hostile population
and of the enemy's cavalry."

A ruined chimney (*left*) marks the approach to Ringgold, Georgia, the jump-off for Sherman's drive on Atlanta. Federal troops had pushed as far as Ringgold, a railroad town 15 miles southeast of Chattanooga, after defeating the Confederates at Lookout Mountain and Missionary Ridge late in 1863.

The road south from Ringgold to the Confederate stronghold at Dalton, Georgia, leads through desolate Mill Creek Gap. The gap was a haven for rough men whose moonshine whiskey, according to photographer George Barnard, was "the worst and cheapest ever made in the state." On May 8, Sherman made a strong feint into the heavily defended gap, then flanked the enemy to the south.

Trees shorn of their branches by
projectiles stand on the battlefield
near Resaca, Georgia, where General
Johnston's Confederates held fast
against the main Federal attack on
May 14. The defenders inflicted
three Union casualties for every two
they suffered, but they were compelled to retreat southward again
after being outflanked.

From these earthworks on high ground outside Resaca, the Confederates repulsed General Sherman's assaults before retiring across the Oostanaula River beyond the town (*left background*). Although the Confederate rear guard set fire to the essential bridges across the river, Sherman's engineers moved in quickly to salvage the spans.

Carefully constructed fortifications at
the Etowah River railroad bridge
were abandoned by the Confederates
on May 20 when Sherman's superior
forces threatened. The defenders
demolished the 620-foot span and retreated to Allatoona Pass. But 600
men of Sherman's construction corps
built a duplicate bridge (*background*) in only six days.

At Allatoona Pass, the railroad to Atlanta snakes through a narrow gorge commanded by a Confederate fort on the hilltop at left. Sherman, who had surveyed the pass 20 years earlier as a young Army lieutenant, knew that a frontal assault would be suicidal. So, on May 23, he swung his forces away from the tracks, south toward the hamlet of Dallas and the crossroads at New Hope Church.

In the Hell Hole, a section of forest near New Hope Church so dense the combatants seldom saw each other, Federals and Confederates met on May 25 and fought to a standoff for more than a week. Bullets and canister rushed through "like a storm-wind," wrote George Barnard of one engagement here. "Tops of trees and heavy branches were falling in splinters among the advancing troops."

At New Hope Church, rifle pits augmented by log traverses enabled infantry on both sides to repulse direct assaults. From these redoubts, marksmen kept up harassing fire on their enemy's exposed camps. "The quiet of the mess-table," reported Barnard, "was invaded by singing Minies that broke crockery and sent scalding coffee into the wide legs of cavalry boots."

A row of Federal gun emplacements
(foreground) crosses a farmer's
field at the base of Little Kennesaw
(rear), one of a string of hills that
shielded nearby Marietta, Georgia,
from Sherman's advance. Beginning
on June 27, Confederate positions
atop these hills withstood nearly a
week of infantry assaults and the
pounding of 140 Union guns, prompt-
ing Sherman to complain that "the
whole country is one vast fort."

From this fortified line on Big Kennesaw, Johnston's Confederate artillery had a superior field of fire on the Federals below. Sherman failed to take the hills, but his assaults occupied the Confederates until a Federal force could maneuver around the enemy flank, forcing Johnston to abandon the Kennesaw line or be cut off from Atlanta, only 18 miles away.

Sherman on the March

"My goodness! I do dread starting out in the dust and hot sun, after such a long period of ease, but the rebels must be whipped, and since we can't do it sitting in the house, I suppose we must content ourselves with going after them."

MAJOR JAMES A. CONNOLLY, 123RD ILLINOIS

On a chilly March day in 1864, two officers in Federal blue stepped aboard a northbound train at Nashville, Tennessee. They were a scruffy-looking pair, so roughhewn in appearance as to mock all the romantic images of gallant and noble captains of war. Both men were indifferently dressed and puffing carelessly on cigars, the ashes from which fell onto their threadbare uniforms.

One officer was average in stature — about five feet eight inches tall and slightly stooped. His companion was three or four inches taller, spare and erect, with nervous hands that kept twitching at his unkempt sandy hair and wiry red beard.

Only the private rail car they were traveling in and the constellation of stars emblazoned on their shoulder straps suggested to bystanders the prominence of the two men.

The shorter of the pair was Ulysses S. Grant, newly promoted to lieutenant general and commander of all the Union armies.

His companion was Major General William Tecumseh Sherman, formerly commander of the Army of the Tennessee and now, effective March 18, Grant's successor as commander of Union forces in the West. Sherman was accompanying his old friend and superior part of the way to Washington in order to discuss strategy.

At Cincinnati the two generals left the train, secreted themselves in a room in the Burnet House, a local hotel, and unfurled their maps. Then Grant began describing his plan for the coming spring offensive.

His plan gave substance to the strategy that President Abraham Lincoln had urged upon his generals in vain virtually since the outbreak of the War three years before. No longer, as Grant wrote later, would the Federal armies in the East and West act "independently and without concert, like a balky team, no two pulling together."

Instead, they would press simultaneously against the Confederacy, said Grant, pounding relentlessly against "a common center." The key thrusts would come in northern Virginia and in northern Georgia. While the Army of the Potomac crossed the Rapidan River and moved south against Robert E. Lee's Army of Northern Virginia, Sherman was to march into Georgia and attack the other major Confederate force, the Army of Tennessee, now commanded by General Joseph E. Johnston.

After two days of talks, Grant traveled on to Washington and Sherman returned to his headquarters in Nashville. There, on April 10, Sherman received a letter from Grant formalizing the plan for the joint spring offensive. "I will stay with the Army of the Potomac and operate directly against Lee's army, wherever it may be found," wrote Grant. "You I propose to move against Johnston's army, to break it up, and to get into the interior of the enemy's country as far as you can, inflicting all the damage you can against their war resources."

Grant did not give Sherman a specific geographical objective. But Sherman interpret-

General William T. Sherman ordered the distribution of corps badges to help identify members of the large and complex force — seven infantry corps and one cavalry in three distinct armies — that he would lead toward Atlanta. The acorn badge denoted XIV Corps of the Army of the Cumberland and the star that army's XX Corps. The arrow was adopted by members of the Army of the Tennessee's XVII Corps.

ed his ultimate target to be Atlanta, which lay more than 100 miles southeast of Chattanooga, site of the resounding Federal victories the year before in November.

Atlanta had become the hub of the Confederate war machine. Sherman had last been in the area when he was a young artillery lieutenant in 1844. The town was then a mere rail hamlet of fewer than 2,000 people and was called Marthasville. Now, swollen to a wartime population of close to 20,000, it was exceeded in importance to the Confederacy only by the capital, Richmond.

Proclaiming itself to be the "Gate City of the South," Atlanta was considered the strategic back door to the seacoast states of the Confederacy. It also served as a vital arsenal and rail center. Atlanta's factories and foundries turned out war matériel of all kinds, from cannon and rifles to rails and armor plate and even uniform buttons and wooden coffins. The four railroads radiating from the city carried these supplies, together with grain and other sustenance from the rich farmlands of Georgia, Alabama and Mississippi, to the principal Confederate armies.

In order to get to Atlanta, Sherman would first have to deal with Joseph Johnston's army, which was entrenched behind a mountain at Dalton, Georgia. And Dalton stood about 30 miles southeast of Chattanooga, squarely athwart the Western & Atlantic Railroad, which was the most direct route to the coveted Gate City.

As Sherman began preparing for his Atlanta Campaign, he was exercising independent command on a large scale for the first time since his disastrous early days of the War in Kentucky. There, during the autumn of 1861, Sherman's responsibilities as commander of the Department of the Cumberland and the fear that he lacked sufficient troops to meet the enemy had led him so perilously close to nervous collapse that some newspapers reported he was insane.

But the subsequent years with Grant — from Shiloh to Vicksburg to Missionary Ridge — had steadied Sherman and had strengthened his confidence. He had come to depend on Grant, and Grant on him. These two Ohio-born generals, unlike in character and temperament, complemented each other. Grant's down-to-earth pragmatism — his "simple faith in success," as Sherman phrased it — balanced Sherman's visionary and intellectual propensities. "We were as brothers," Sherman wrote later. "I the older man in years, he the higher in rank."

Sherman described that kinship in blunter terms on another occasion. "He stood by me when I was crazy," he said, "and I stood by him when he was drunk; and now we stand by each other always."

At the age of 44, Sherman was on his own again — and under orders to be ready to march by the end of April. He believed that preparation was virtually everything. "The least part of a general's work," he said, "is to fight a battle." And he had only a month to prepare, to focus all his prodigious mental energies, to harness the brilliant but erratic mind that someone said "perspired thought at every pore."

Sherman's first task, undertaken in late March, was to inspect his command. His Military Division of the Mississippi embraced three major forces — the Armies of the Cumberland, the Tennessee and the Ohio — scattered about the state of Tennessee and extending into northern Alabama and Mississippi. These armies would field a fighting force of about 100,000 troops — nearly double the enemy's numbers at Dalton — for the march against Atlanta.

For the most part, these were veteran troops. Many already had signed up for another three-year tour of duty, motivated variously by patriotism, by bounties and by the exhortations of unit commanders who backed up their speeches with liberal rations of whiskey.

The troops were also well rested. Except for a Sherman-led raid in February that ripped up 16 miles of enemy railroad around Meridian, Mississippi, and a simultaneous demonstration against the Confederates at Dalton, they had spent the months since November in winter quarters. Many had even had a month at home on furlough.

Nevertheless, Sherman faced a mammoth problem: making provision for supplying his troops on the march.

His supplies first had to be brought to Chattanooga over the single ribbon of rails that ran more than 300 miles to his rear: 150 miles northwest to Nashville and then 185 miles farther north to the main depot at Louisville. Although Grant since February had made much progress repairing and securing the railroad, the slender life line was still vulnerable along its entire length to slashing at-

A photograph taken in late 1863 shows Ulysses S. Grant shortly before he gained another star, becoming the first officer since George Washington to hold the full grade of lieutenant general in the U.S. Army. Grant's great virtues, according to his friend and trusted subordinate William Tecumseh Sherman *(far right)*, were "simplicity of character, singleness of purpose."

Generals and staff officers of the veteran XIV Corps of the Army of the Cumberland gather for a photograph shortly before Sherman sent them toward Atlanta in May 1864. The march into Georgia was spearheaded at times by the corps' 2nd Division, led by Brigadier General Jefferson C. Davis, who sits at far left.

General William T. Sherman, one of his soldiers asserted, was "the most American-looking man I ever saw." In addition to "a sharp, prominent red nose," Sherman had "a rusty beard trimmed close" and "small bright eyes." The same soldier described Sherman as "boiling over with ideas while discussing every subject and pronouncing on all."

tacks by local guerrillas and by Confederate cavalrymen such as the legendary Nathan Bedford Forrest.

The threat posed by Forrest became a reality even as Sherman began bolstering the railroads for the Atlanta Campaign. On April 12, out in western Tennessee, a cavalry division led by Forrest overwhelmed the small Federal outpost called Fort Pillow, killing about 230 defenders, including many soldiers — the majority were black — who were massacred after the garrison surrendered.

To protect the railroads in the rear against the man Sherman referred to as "that devil Forrest," Sherman ordered the construction of additional blockhouses at important bridges and tunnels. Between the strong points, at eight-mile intervals, sidings would be built to expedite traffic, and each siding would be manned by a telegraph operator to provide warning of enemy attacks.

Anticipating that some disruption would be inevitable, Sherman instituted a training program for his rail-repair gangs. These teams of gandy dancers went through daily drills as rigorous as those required of riflemen and gun crews, practicing methods of replacing the rails as rapidly as the enemy ripped them up.

Sherman's best insurance against rail disruption in the rear was to stockpile munitions and rations as far forward as possible — at Chattanooga and at Nashville, where 12 new warehouses were under construction. In order to free enough rail cars to accumulate supplies at Nashville and Chattanooga, Sherman issued a series of orders drastically restricting traffic on the railroad. Troops returning from furloughs in the North, for example, were barred from taking trains. Instead, they were formed into detachments to

march south, driving herds of cattle for Sherman's armies as they went.

These returning soldiers had no recourse, but when Sherman banned all civilian rail traffic south of Nashville, howls of protest went up. The loudest cries came from newspaper reporters, for the ban effectively prevented them from traveling to Chattanooga to cover the impending Federal advance — unless, of course, they wanted to walk.

The prospect of campaigning without any newspaper coverage delighted Sherman, who loathed all reporters except those few willing to volunteer for combat service with his armies. He believed that any reporting about his forces aided the enemy. In fact, at Vicksburg the previous year, he had actually court-martialed a newspaper correspondent for publishing stories that allegedly revealed Federal troop movements to the enemy.

Sherman was just as tough with most other civilians who disputed his ban on rail travel. When religious groups complained that his orders kept them from shipping Biblical tracts to the troops, he snapped: "There is more need of gunpowder and oats than any moral or religious instruction."

He stood firm even when the complaints of loyal residents in eastern Tennessee, who depended upon the railroad for food, drew a response from the President. To Lincoln's request that he do something "for those suffering people," Sherman replied that either those people or the army "must quit and the army don't intend to unless Joe Johnston makes us. I will not change my order."

Sherman proved willing to bend his orders, however, for at least one noncombatant. He had a soft spot for Mary Ann Bickerdyke, the renowned Mother Bickerdyke, who been following the Western armies for

Slaughter at Fort Pillow

In the spring of 1864, a minor Federal outpost in Tennessee called Fort Pillow became a byword for senseless brutality. Situated atop a bluff guarding the Mississippi River about 75 miles north of Memphis, the fort was garrisoned by about 550 Federal troops, almost half of them recently recruited blacks. On April 12, around 1,500 of General Nathan Bedford Forrest's Confederate cavalrymen stormed the fort as part of a campaign to cut Union lines of communication. The yelling troopers swarmed over the fort's parapets and swiftly drove many of the defenders down the bluff toward the Mississippi.

What happened next was soon the subject of rancorous debate. Forrest's men maintained that the Federals, although fleeing, kept their weapons and frequently turned to shoot, forcing the Confederates to keep firing. Surviving members of the garrison, on the other hand, said that most of their men surrendered and threw down their arms — only to be shot or bayoneted in cold blood by the attackers, who repeatedly shouted, "No quarter! No quarter!"

Doubtless some of the Federals did continue to fight. But it seems clear from the casualty figures alone that a post-surrender massacre took place. Only 14 of Forrest's men were killed, but the Federals lost about 230 dead and 100 more seriously wounded, a huge number considering the fact that the Confederate assault was so swiftly victorious. Further, a large majority of the Federal dead were black troops — an indication that the Confederate soldiers had taken vengeance on former slaves fighting in the Union's cause.

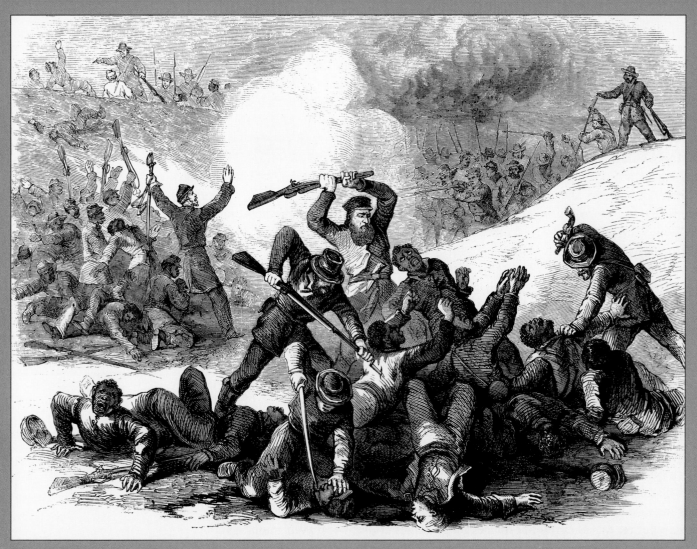

A New York magazine illustration gives a grisly version of the Fort Pillow incident with Confederates clubbing, stabbing and shooting helpless Federals.

almost three years as a volunteer nurse.

When Mother Bickerdyke was told of Sherman's ban, she set out to subvert it. First, she managed to get her supply of food and bandages from Nashville to Chattanooga by concealing them in a wagon train of army ambulances. Then she went to the Nashville station and bullied her way onto the next train for Chattanooga.

She hurried to Sherman's new headquarters, bustled past his aides and confronted the commanding general. Sherman would have to change his orders, she announced, so that her hospital supplies could reach the front on the railroad.

"Well," said Sherman, "I'm busy today."

"No," Mother Bickerdyke insisted, "fix this thing as it ought to be fixed. Have some sense about it."

Sherman laughed and then attempted to joke with her.

"Well," she said at length, "I can't stand fooling here all day. Write an order for two cars a day."

Sherman did as she said. Later, when some of his officers complained about Mother Bickerdyke, Sherman threw up his hands and said, "She outranks me. I can't do a thing in the world."

By standing tough against most complainers, Sherman quickly managed nearly to double the accumulation of stores at forward depots. But this was not good enough. The trains at his command — approximately 60 locomotives and 600 cars — were too few to meet his goal of bringing 130 carloads of supplies forward daily.

His solution was patently Shermanesque. He instructed his transportation chief to seize and hold all trains arriving at Nashville from Louisville. In this manner he could

A strong-willed widow from Galesburg, Illinois, Mary Ann Bickerdyke rode roughshod over any Federal officers who tried to interfere with her self-assigned nursing duties. When a surgeon asked her by whose authority she was working in his hospital, Mother Bickerdyke replied, "I have received my authority from the Lord God Almighty. Have you any higher authority?"

amass the fleet of 100 engines and 1,000 cars he needed. Soon, supply-laden rolling stock was chugging into Chattanooga.

Sherman accomplished all this with characteristic personal intensity. Sleeping only three or four hours a night, he seemed to be everywhere, barking out orders, twisting his face as if in pain, tugging at scalp or beard, tapping his fingers restlessly, exhausting subordinates with his kinetic presence.

Sherman would become so preoccupied with the problem at hand, a Pennsylvanian remembered, that he was known "to demand of a soldier a light from a pipe for his cigar, and then to dash the pipe on the ground as if it were a match, and rush away unconscious of the soldier's surprise and the meaning of the laughter of the bystanders."

Sherman hounded his quartermaster relentlessly, demanding more of everything. The slow and the incompetent felt the lash of his tongue. "I'm going to move on Joe Johnston the day Grant telegraphs me he is going to hit Bobby Lee," he raged at one quartermaster, "and if you don't have my army supplied, and keep it supplied, we'll eat your mules up, sir — eat your mules up!"

At the same time, Sherman hedged his bets by preparing alternative plans for feeding his forces. He carefully studied the tax documents and census reports of every county in Georgia, looking for the best places to live off the land in case the rail supply line failed to keep pace with his advance. "Georgia has a million of inhabitants," he wrote Grant on April 10. "If they can live, we should not starve."

Sherman had no qualms that foraging might somehow be considered unchivalrous. A few months before in Nashville, dining at the home of the mother-in-law of one of his generals, he had listened impatiently while the hostess condemned his soldiers for taking food from the countryside.

"Madam," he replied, "my soldiers have to subsist themselves even if the whole country must be ruined to maintain them. War is cruelty. There is no use trying to reform it; the crueler it is, the sooner it will be over."

While Sherman completed his preparations, his adversary at Dalton, 30 miles away, faced an even larger challenge. General Joseph Johnston and his Confederate Army of Tennessee also depended upon supply by rail — specifically the Western & Atlantic Railroad from Atlanta. The area around Dalton had few farms; it was a mountainous, river-laced wilderness.

Unlike Sherman, however, Johnston did not have the authority to seize control of his life line. The State of Georgia owned the Western & Atlantic; because of mismanagement and the shortage of rolling stock, a single trainload of supplies sometimes took up to 36 hours to move over the 85-mile run from Atlanta to Dalton.

But Johnston faced problems bigger than logistics. When he had taken command at Dalton the previous December, replacing Braxton Bragg, who resigned after the defeat

at Chattanooga, Johnston found a demoralized army of about 43,000 men. The army had been so shattered by the losses at Lookout Mountain and Missionary Ridge that soldiers were deserting by the thousands.

The lack of manpower was so desperate that just a few days after Johnston's arrival in Dalton one of his most respected division commanders, Major General Patrick Cleburne, submitted a startling proposal signed by 13 of his brigade and regimental officers. In order to gain thousands of new recruits, Cleburne suggested, the Confederacy ought to enlist slaves as soldiers and reward them with emancipation.

The very idea shocked Johnston and most of his subordinate generals. One officer, apparently with an eye to discrediting Cleburne, forwarded a copy of the proposal to the government at Richmond. President Jefferson Davis thereupon so effectively suppressed all traces of Cleburne's document that it did not surface again until 25 years after the War.

Johnston brought impressive credentials to the difficulties of his new command. Early in the War, he had led what was now renowned as the Army of Northern Virginia until severe wounds — suffered in May 1862 at Fair Oaks, near Richmond — put him out of action, paving the way for his old West Point classmate, Robert E. Lee. Since November 1862, Johnston had served in the prestigious but largely powerless post of chief of the Department of the West.

Moreover, Johnston looked and acted like a leader. He was in his mid-50s, compactly built, with a gray goatee and closely cropped side whiskers. His quiet good manners and his jaunty appearance made an immediate impression on the troops. "His hat was deco-

rated with a star and feather, and he wore a bright new sash, big gauntlets, and silver spurs," remembered Private Sam Watkins of the 1st Tennessee. "He was the very picture of a general."

To deal with the problem of desertions, Johnston adopted a carrot-and-stick approach. He proclaimed a general amnesty for deserters who agreed to return to the ranks, and to help prevent further unauthorized absences he started a program of furloughs that enabled every man to go home for a brief period. But Johnston also made terrible examples of incorrigible offenders: He stood them up at the foot of freshly dug graves and had them shot in front of the entire army.

Johnston organized his seven infantry divisions into two corps. One was led by Lieutenant General William J. Hardee, the vet-eran corps commander who, at 48, had been rejuvenated by a recent marriage to a delicate Alabama beauty who was young enough to be his daughter.

The other corps went to a new arrival — the celebrated and badly crippled John Bell Hood, whose left arm had been shattered at Gettysburg and whose right leg had been lost at Chickamauga. Hood joined Johnston in February fresh from a long convalescence in Richmond, where he had been lionized and promoted — at the age of 32 — to lieutenant general.

Johnston and his corps commanders put the army through intensive and sometimes innovative training. Patrick Cleburne had a log cabin built and conducted classes in tactics there for his brigade commanders, who instructed regimental officers, who in

In an impressive display of military muscle, two full brigades of the Federal IV Corps maneuver during training exercises near Chattanooga. Skirmishers lead waves of double-ranked infantry across the field while artillery pieces draw up to give support. The IV Corps was part of General George Thomas' Army of the Cumberland, largest of the armies that Sherman would lead into Georgia.

reverently as "Old Joe." One young cavalry captain wrote home in April that Johnston "seems to have infused a new spirit into the whole mass, and out of chaos brought order and beauty." Many years later, Private Sam Watkins recalled: "He was loved, respected, admired; yea, almost worshipped by his troops."

Johnston inspired considerably less respect among his superiors in Richmond. He had been at odds with President Davis ever since the first summer of the War, when a dispute over Johnston's seniority deeply wounded the general's fierce pride. Davis, in turn, resented Johnston's failure to explain to him his plans for withdrawing his army from Manassas to the outskirts of Richmond during the spring of 1862.

Davis so distrusted Johnston's ability, in fact, that back in December he had frantically looked elsewhere for someone to command the Army of Tennessee. He had even offered the post to Lee, who refused it in favor of remaining in command of the Army of Northern Virginia.

Having settled on Johnston — with "doubt and misgiving," according to his Secretary of War, James A. Seddon — Davis and other officials began bombarding the new commander with suggestions. They wanted him to take the offensive by striking into eastern Tennessee.

Richmond's expectations were unrealistic, and Johnston parried them. Citing the lack of wagons, the risk of being cut off from his Georgia base of supply and, above all, the numerical superiority of 2 to 1 enjoyed by the Federals in Tennessee, Johnston rightly insisted that the army was too weak for such a campaign.

Davis doubted Johnston's gloomy assess-

turn taught company commanders. Johnston's cavalry chief, Major General Joseph Wheeler, drilled his horsemen in the art of charging an infantry line: He lined up dummies made of old clothes stuffed with straw and then had his troopers charge at full speed, sabers held high all the while, under fire from blank cartridges.

Together with Hardee and Hood, Johnston repeatedly reviewed the army on parade. Hundreds of spectators rode up from Atlanta to watch these parades and to witness exciting sham battles that pitted division against division.

Johnston also watched out for his soldiers' welfare. He somehow managed to provide shoes, extra food, and a ration of whiskey and tobacco twice a week for the troops; in turn, they idolized him, referring to him ment. For one thing, the President was getting quite a different story from one of Johnston's own top generals. During March and April, John Bell Hood sent Richmond a series of secret and highly optimistic reports. "The enemy is weak and we are strong" went the typical Hood refrain.

It was just what the President wanted to hear. Hood, though so handicapped physically that he had to be strapped into the saddle, had evidently lost neither his zest for carrying the War to the enemy nor his ambition for even higher rank. Intentionally or not, Hood was bolstering his own standing with Davis and undermining whatever confidence the Confederate President may have retained in Johnston.

Unaware of Hood's clandestine campaign, Johnston maintained friendly relations with the young general. Characteristically, however, Johnston kept his own counsel, revealing little of his plans for the coming months to either Hood or the government.

But anyone familiar with Johnston's tactics earlier in the War could have made an educated guess at his intentions in north Georgia. On the battlegrounds of Virginia, Johnston had demonstrated a marked preference for the defense and the quick counterpunch over the attack. And these would be his tactics at Dalton.

The Confederate position at Dalton appeared at first glance to be ideal for such moves. A series of ridges stood between Dalton and any Federal advance from Chattanooga. The nearest of these to the defenders, Rocky Face Ridge, was only a few miles west of Dalton. It provided a virtually impregnable shield of sheer rock that reared 800 feet above the valley floor and extended on a north-south axis for about 20 miles.

Patient and friendly with his troops, General Joseph E. Johnston could be curt with his superiors. When Confederate President Jefferson Davis urged him to attack Sherman's force, Johnston listed some obstacles to an offensive with acid brevity: "Chattanooga, now a fortress, the Tennessee River, the rugged desert of the Cumberland Mountains, and an army outnumbering ours by more than two to one."

Johnston fortified Rocky Face Ridge and fixed his mind firmly on the defensive. He He would wait for the high-strung Sherman to commit a blunder. Then he would attack. Of these plans Johnston told the President only: "I can see no other mode of taking the offensive here than to beat the enemy when he advances and then move forward."

Then, at the end of April, a spate of alarming reports from Johnston's cavalry scouts rendered academic any comment from Richmond. The unseasonably cold spring had suddenly turned warm, and the Federal armies were reported to be on the move in a wide arc toward Dalton.

On May 1, a lovely Sunday with the trees bursting into full foliage, Johnston sounded the alert. He put his officers' wives on the train for Atlanta and wired Richmond asking for reinforcements. His army now counted nearly 45,000 men present for duty, but he needed more.

The government responded by instructing Lieutenant General Leonidas Polk in Alabama to send a division and whatever else he could spare. Officials hesitated to order up additional reinforcements. They suspected that Grant was about to take the offensive in Virginia, and they refused to believe that the Federals finally intended to wage full-scale war on two fronts at once.

On that same beautiful Sunday, William Sherman rode a few miles out from Chattanooga and picked bouquets of wild flowers from the deserted battlefield at Missionary Ridge. He mailed the bouquets to his daughters, Minnie and Lizzie, so that — as he wrote them that day — "both of you will have a present to commemorate this bright opening of spring."

For these few hours at least, Sherman felt at peace with himself. His preparations for the offensive were complete. To the astonishment of veteran railroad men, his supply line had achieved a rate as high as 193 carloads a day. His depots in Nashville and Chattanooga bulged with rations and ammunition enough to sustain his armies in the field for more than four months.

And by rail and road, his armies were on the move. The Army of the Cumberland, 60,733 men under Major General George H. Thomas, was in the center, concentrating around the Georgia rail station of Ringgold, about midway to Dalton on the Western & Atlantic Railroad.

The Army of the Tennessee, 24,465 men under Major General James B. McPherson, was on the Federal right, moving toward Chattanooga from northern Alabama, soon to turn southeast on a route roughly parallel with Thomas'.

The Army of the Ohio, 13,559 men under Major General John M. Schofield, was on the Federal left, marching due south via the Tennessee town of Cleveland and following another railroad — the East Tennessee & Georgia — which joined the Western & Atlantic at Dalton.

By Sherman's strict orders, all three armies were stripped down for action. Sherman wanted his fighting force to be "a mobile machine, willing and able to start at a minute's notice, and to subsist on the scantiest food."

The wagon trains allotted to each division carried supplies for 20 days. Each regiment was limited to one baggage wagon and one ambulance. The officers in a company could take but one pack mule among them. Large field tents were discouraged except for the sick and wounded and to serve as an office for each regimental headquarters.

Every soldier was under orders to carry three days' rations — and to make them last for five days. By Sherman's reckoning, each of his seven infantry corps thus bore on the backs of its men enough supplies to eliminate 300 wagons.

Sherman himself set a spartan example. His entire field headquarters of aides, clerks and orderlies made do with a single wagon. Sherman stuffed all his official papers in his pocket, later filing them away in an empty candle box. "I think that is as low down as we can get," he said, "until we get flat broke."

In the wake of his marching armies, he left Chattanooga and rode into Georgia on May 5 — the same day that Grant, having crossed the Rapidan with the Army of the Potomac, launched his offensive in northern Virginia. The armies of the East and West were pulling together at last. On battlefields nearly 600 miles apart, the strategy that Grant and Sherman had mapped six weeks before in a Cincinnati hotel room would now be put to the test.

Two days later, from his forward base at Ringgold, General Sherman formally launched the campaign against Atlanta. Early on the morning of May 7, the vanguard of Thomas' Army of the Cumberland attacked the Confederate outpost at Tunnel Hill, a ridge seven miles southeast of Ringgold.

Here, where the Western & Atlantic tunneled through the ridge, a Federal battle line more than a mile long confronted three thin brigades of Confederate cavalry. The defenders, fighting dismounted behind breastworks with support from horse artillery, delayed the Federals for a couple of hours but then fell back so rapidly that they neglected to destroy the tunnel.

A few miles farther down the railroad, the Federal advance came up against the main Confederate line at Rocky Face Ridge. The west face of the ridge rose almost vertically in a craggy wall of quartz. On the knife-edge crest, Confederate officers sipped water from their canteens and gestured smugly to the mass of Federals far below them.

Only one major pass breached Rocky Face. Through this gateway, Mill Creek Gap, the railroad mounted the ridge and then descended to Dalton just beyond. But Confederate engineers had flooded much of the gap by damming Mill Creek. The reservoir they created was 16 feet deep in places and flanked by earthworks. And the gap itself was dominated by towering cliffs that bore the ominous name Buzzard's Roost and bristled with cannon and grayclad infantry.

Sherman, glimpsing all this through a glass from atop Tunnel Hill, saw the gap as a "terrible door of death." He had no intention of attempting to enter it. He would merely pretend to.

In a masquerade Sherman planned for Joseph Johnston's benefit, two Federal armies would act as decoys. Thomas' Army of the Cumberland, confronting Rocky Face from the west, would feign an aggressive assault on that ridge. From the north, Schofield's Army of the Ohio would demonstrate at the northern terminus of the ridge, where its right linked up at a 90-degree angle with Thomas' troops and its left extended to the east across Crow Valley.

Sherman's script called for the real drama to take place farther south and to star McPherson's Army of the Tennessee. McPherson was already engaged in a wide flanking maneuver, marching in a southeasterly direction toward the little town of Villanow. From there he was to slip through Snake Creek Gap, a long defile that separated the impenetrable Rocky Face from a ridge to the south. Then McPherson would march east and strike the railroad in the Confederate rear at Resaca, 15 miles south of Dalton, severing Johnston's life line.

When that happened, Sherman reasoned, his enemy would have to withdraw south from Dalton. Then McPherson could hit the Confederates in flank while the other two Federal armies crossed Rocky Face unopposed and pursued Johnston from the north.

The basic idea for this plan, which held promise of ending the campaign before it had scarcely begun, came from George Thomas. He had thought of it back in February when his army felt out the enemy defenses at Rocky Face in support of Sherman's raid in Mississippi. In proposing it to Sherman,

Perched inside a bandstand that resembles a huge bird's nest, the regimental band of the 38th Illinois prepares to serenade Brigadier General William P. Carlin *(center, double row of buttons)* and his staff; Carlin's brigade was posted near Ringgold, Georgia, preparing to march on Atlanta. Carlin would lead his men so effectively during the upcoming campaign that he would be promoted to command of a division.

Thomas wanted his army to carry out the flanking maneuver.

But Sherman insisted that his own old Army of the Tennessee — "my whiplash," he called it — was faster on its feet. Thomas' Army of the Cumberland, nearly three times as large, had the reputation of being resolute in battle but slow and cumbersome — not unlike the methodical Thomas himself. Sherman wanted to keep that massive force of Cumberlanders in front of Rocky Face, between the Confederates and Chattanooga, just in case Johnston decided to attack.

Sherman may have had another reason as well for selecting the Army of the Tennessee to play the pivotal role. McPherson was a fellow Ohioan, an old friend and a favorite of both Grant's and Sherman's. A handsome and engaging six-footer, first in his class at West Point, the 35-year-old McPherson clearly was headed for higher command. "If

he lives," Sherman said, "he'll outdistance Grant and myself."

Thomas took Sherman's decision with his usual stoicism. He made no show of pique, just as he had not complained back in March when Grant passed over him on the seniority list and appointed Sherman to the Western command.

Sherman appreciated this quality in his old West Point roommate. At Tunnel Hill, he looked the other way when Thomas set up an elaborate field headquarters with so many tents that Sherman laughingly but affectionately called it "Thomasville." But more important, Sherman knew, was that Thomas would loyally carry out his orders to "occupy the attention of all the enemy" while McPherson skirted south of Rocky Face.

On Sunday, May 8, Thomas' army and Schofield's Army of the Ohio probed for the weakest places in the Confederate defenses at

Men of the 154th New York — the vanguard of General John Geary's division — make a futile charge up Confederate-held Rocky Face Ridge. Colonel Patrick Henry Jones (*above*), commander of the 154th, suffered injuries when he fell from the sheer rock face but recovered to fight again during the Atlanta Campaign.

Rocky Face. The main Confederate line began about a mile south of Mill Creek Gap, extended north for a couple of miles and then bent eastward at a right angle to cover Crow Valley, north of Dalton.

That morning, Thomas sent one division scrambling up the lightly defended northern end of Rocky Face, where the slope was least precipitous. These soldiers, supported by one of Schofield's divisions, worked their way south for about a mile on a crest so narrow it would permit passage of no more than four men abreast. About a third of the way to Mill Creek Gap, they were forced to halt under heavy fire from the Confederate main line, which was shielded by stone breastworks, and begin piling up boulders of their own for protection.

In the meantime, that afternoon another of Thomas' divisions staged a strong demonstration at a point about four miles south of Mill Creek Gap. Here, a slight depression known as Dug Gap had been gouged out of the mountain to permit the passage of a country road. Dug Gap lay to the south of the main Confederate defenses and was guarded by a force of only about 1,000 men — two Arkansas regiments and a small brigade of Kentucky cavalry commanded by Colonel J. Warren Grigsby.

About 3 p.m. the Federal division commander, Brigadier General John W. Geary, deployed two full brigades at the base of Dug Gap and started them up the ridge. At first, moving through thick woods and rocky outcroppings, the Federals met only Confederate skirmishers who quickly retreated back up the mountain.

Nearing the top, however, Geary's men encountered an awesome obstacle. Looming above them, the crest consisted of a palisade of rock that was "almost perpendicular," recalled Lieutenant Stephen Pierson of the 33rd New Jersey. "It was 15 or 20 feet high and pierced by some narrow crevices, through which but a single man could pass at a time. Through these crevices we saw their skirmishers pass, and then their main line opened furiously upon us, and added to our confusion by sending from the top great boulders rolling down the mountain side."

From this stronghold, the Confederate defenders — using the boulders to supplement their dwindling supply of ammunition — stubbornly held their ground despite a Federal numerical superiority of more than 4 to 1. Toward evening, the Confederates got help: Two brigades of infantry under General Patrick Cleburne hurried out from Dalton. Cleburne rode on ahead of his troops, accompanied by the corps commander himself, William Hardee.

As Cleburne's column reached the eastern base of the ridge, the brigade of Texans in the lead made a happy discovery. The Kentucky cavalrymen who were fighting up in the gap had left their horses down below. The footsore Texans jumped on the mounts and, with many of them riding double, galloped whooping and shouting up the mountainside.

The first Texan to reach the crest rode up to where Cleburne and Hardee were watching the progress of the battle. He dismounted, saluted with a flourish and asked, "Where am I most needed?" The two generals looked at the boy in disbelief and then burst into laughter.

By then, it was getting dark, and Geary's Federals were already beginning to withdraw down the mountain. Their demonstration had proved costly: Geary reported losses of 357 men. Confederate casualties were perhaps one fifth that number.

But the demonstration also proved effective. While Geary kept the Confederates occupied at Dug Gap, McPherson's Army of the Tennessee was marching unmolested from Villanow, a half dozen miles to the southwest. McPherson's leading elements reached the western entrance to Snake Creek Gap that night just about the same time Geary's brigades were withdrawing down Rocky Face.

Incredibly, the Confederates had failed to guard this six-mile-long defile, which pointed like an arrow toward their rear at Resaca. McPherson's men occupied it without firing a shot and camped there that Sunday night secure in its thickly wooded wilderness.

During the night, someone in Confederate headquarters at Dalton belatedly realized that Snake Creek Gap was undefended and ordered a brigade of cavalry there to stand guard over the passage. The assignment was given to Colonel Grigsby's Kentucky troopers, who had been so effective in helping to defend Dug Gap.

It was after dawn on Monday when they approached the eastern entrance to Snake Creek Gap — too late. Just then, McPherson's army began to emerge from the gap into Sugar Valley with the 9th Illinois Mounted Infantry in the lead. The Kentuckians opened fire on the 9th Illinois and managed to stop the Federal advance for a moment or two. But then blueclad infantry moved at the double-quick to the head of the

In a probing attack that was intended to pin down General Joseph Johnston's Confederates, Federal troops from General George Thomas' Army of the Cumberland skirmish in Mill Creek Gap, where the tracks of the Western & Atlantic Railroad cross Rocky Face Ridge.

column and forced Grigsby's troopers back toward Resaca.

At 12:30 p.m., McPherson started a messenger to Sherman with the news that he was only five miles from Resaca — his advance elements much closer — with no real opposition in sight.

Back at his headquarters at Tunnel Hill, Sherman awaited word of his protégé's progress with what one observer described as "electric alertness." Everything else was going according to plan. On the northern summit of Rocky Face and farther south at "the terrible door of death," Sherman's two remaining armies had successfully occupied the Confederates' attention. The railroad was operating on schedule. With Federal work crews repairing the tracks in front of the locomotive, the first trainload of supplies from Chattanooga arrived that day at the Tunnel Hill station.

Sherman was sitting down to supper late that afternoon when the message from McPherson finally arrived. He read it with increasing excitement. If McPherson had been five miles from Resaca at 12:30, Sherman reasoned, then the Army of the Tennessee must have reached there by this time and already begun ripping up the Confederates' railroad life line.

Sherman could hardly contain his joy. He hammered his fist on the table until the supper dishes rattled, and he shouted: "I've got Joe Johnston dead!"

Into the "Hell Hole"

"We have struck a hornet nest at the business end."

PRIVATE ALLAN FAHNSTOCK, U.S.A., AT THE BATTLE OF NEW HOPE CHURCH

Joseph Johnston passed that Monday afternoon at his headquarters in Dalton quite unaware of the threat to his rear. He was looking to the north for trouble, not to the south and Resaca.

From the beginning of the campaign, Johnston had expected the main Federal attack on Dalton to come down the open avenue of Crow Valley along the East Tennessee & Georgia Railroad, and he had concentrated the bulk of his forces there. He was surprised when the Federals kept popping up not only on the north but on the west as well, along the length of Rocky Face Ridge. Now McPherson and his Army of the Tennessee were marching on Resaca and Johnston did not even know it.

But for all his ignorance about Sherman's intentions, Johnston was also the recipient of a piece of extraordinarily good fortune. The vanguard of General Leonidas Polk's reinforcements—a 4,000-man division under Brigadier General James Cantey—had come to Resaca by train on Saturday and Johnston had ordered it to remain there.

Thus, as McPherson moved east through Sugar Valley with no apparent opposition on Monday afternoon, a rude surprise awaited the young general. In midafternoon the head of McPherson's column encountered some of Cantey's Confederate skirmishers stationed on a hill about a mile west of Resaca. Federal skirmishers cleared the hill, and McPherson deployed one of his two corps and brought the other up in support.

This took more than two hours, and it was well after 5 p.m. when McPherson decided to take a firsthand look at the enemy before ordering a full-scale assault. He rode up the hill, mounted a tree stump and scanned the Confederate line through a glass while his conspicuous six-foot frame attracted Confederate artillery fire.

McPherson did not like what he saw: The Confederates—presumably in great numbers—were well fortified on the heights in front of Resaca, supported by artillery and protected by the swampy bottoms of Camp Creek, which separated the enemy forces. Though the Federals had a manpower advantage of nearly 5 to 1, McPherson did not know it. Moreover, only an hour of daylight remained.

McPherson stepped down from the stump and decided not to risk an assault. After dark, his men lit bonfires to mask the withdrawal. Then the entire army marched back to Snake Creek Gap and bivouacked there. Only an 18-man detachment of mounted infantry from the 9th Illinois had reached the railroad. They swung north of Resaca and managed to cut the telegraph wires, but not the rails, before being driven off.

McPherson later explained that if he had attacked or remained in front of Resaca that night, Johnston would have swept down on his vulnerable left flank from Dalton and cut off his army "as you cut off the end of a piece of tape with a pair of shears."

During the night, in fact, three Confederate divisions under John Bell Hood did arrive at the outskirts of Resaca. Johnston had

A member of the 15th Ohio color guard carries the flag over the bodies of his comrades at Pickett's Mill on May 27, 1864; no fewer than six of the regiment's color-bearers fell that day. The action bore out the words of John Palmer, commander of the Federal XIV Corps, who had written home from Rome, Georgia, the week before: "We are still 53 miles from Atlanta. We will have some bloody work before we enter that place."

ordered them there from Dalton Monday evening when he learned at last of McPherson's presence in Sugar Valley. But when Hood found that McPherson had retired to Snake Creek Gap, Johnston recalled one of the divisions and brought the other two back as far as Tilton Station, there to keep watch midway between Dalton and Resaca.

Early Tuesday morning, Sherman got the stunning news of McPherson's withdrawal. He was "much vexed," according to one witness. His favorite army and his most trusted general had failed him. They "could have walked into Resaca," he wrote after the War, but "at the critical moment McPherson seems to have been a little cautious." The next time he saw McPherson, however, Sherman said simply, "Well, Mac, you have missed the opportunity of your life."

Sherman sent word to McPherson to stay put in Snake Creek Gap, and then he worked out a new plan. This time Sherman adopted George Thomas' original idea of flanking Dalton with a much larger force. Leaving one corps to maintain the demonstration in front of Rocky Face Ridge, he would move the rest of his forces south and through the gap. Then, as he reported to Washington that night, he would place those troops "between Johnston and Resaca, when we will have to fight it out."

Sherman was in no hurry. Before carrying out the march to the gap, he intended to wait for a division of cavalry — approximately 3,000 men under Brigadier General George Stoneman — en route from Tennessee and not expected for two days. He needed Stoneman to protect his left flank when the Army of the Ohio moved out. Meanwhile, he was counting on the enemy to remain at Dalton.

Joseph Johnston unwittingly went along with Sherman's plan. He was not worried about Resaca. McPherson's thrust there, he concluded, was merely a feint designed to divert attention from the attack he still expected to come from north of Dalton.

In any event, Resaca appeared secure. Major General William W. Loring's division of reinforcements from Mississippi was pouring in there to join Cantey's men, and another division was now within easy supporting distance. And on Wednesday, May 11, Leonidas Polk arrived to take charge of the defenses at Resaca.

Polk, the 58-year-old "bishop-general," was a West Pointer who had entered the ministry, become Episcopal bishop of Louisiana and, in 1861, taken up his sword again. That night, riding the train up to Dalton in the company of John Bell Hood, Polk was pleased to find need of his prewar vocation. Hood confided his wish to be baptized into the Church.

At Dalton, after meeting with his old friend Johnston, Polk went to Hood's headquarters about midnight. There, while the one-legged Hood, unable to kneel, leaned on his crutches in the dim candlelight, the portly bishop dipped his hands into a horse bucket of consecrated water and performed the rite of baptism. Then he buckled on his sword and returned to Resaca.

Even with Polk now covering the rear, Johnston nevertheless began to feel uneasy. Worried by reports of enemy movements on the far side of Rocky Face, he ordered Major General Joseph Wheeler at dawn on Thursday, May 12, to take all his available cavalry around the northern tip of the ridge and find out what Sherman was up to. All Wheeler found was Stoneman's Federal cavalry. The Federal infantry, except for Thomas' IV

Corps, which was still in place west of the ridge, had departed for Snake Creek Gap.

Johnston, aware at last of the real threat to his rear, abandoned Dalton that night. The withdrawal began about 1 a.m. and went smoothly. Johnston, the master of retreat, was prepared: He sent his columns toward Resaca on routes designated in advance; the troops were accompanied by local guides.

Johnston reached Resaca with his army on the morning of Friday the 13th — just in time. Even as his men filed into position, the Federal armies were massing in Sugar Valley and sending skirmishers toward Resaca.

Polk was on the job in his customary battle garb of slouch hat and old gray hunting shirt. Polk's men held off the Federals long enough for Johnston to bolster the lines on the high ground commanding Camp Creek west of Resaca. These defenses formed a four-mile-long arc, anchored on the left at the Oostanaula River, just below the hamlet, and on the right at the Conasauga, a tributary of the Oostanaula east of the railroad.

Johnston had the high ground — and better numerical odds than before. With the arrival of most of Polk's men, who now constituted a third corps of infantry, he could count about 66,000 men. Sherman, with the addition of Stoneman's cavalry, numbered approximately 104,000.

Sherman himself stayed up late on the 13th mapping his tactics. In fact, he was so sleepy the next morning that, riding toward the front, he stopped to catnap. A soldier passing by saw him slumped against a tree and inquired of an orderly who stood nearby, "Is that a general?"

Told that it was, the soldier said angrily, "A pretty way we're commanded when our

Lieutenant General Leonidas Polk, one of Joseph Johnston's corps commanders, was roundly criticized in the North for combining his duties as an Episcopalian bishop with those of a Confederate officer. To loyal Southerners, though, Polk's wartime mission seemed divinely sanctioned. "Like Gideon and David," the Memphis *Appeal* proclaimed, "he is marshaling his legions to fight the battle of the Lord."

generals are lying drunk beside the road!"

"Stop, my man!" shouted Sherman, leaping to his feet. "I'm not drunk. While you were sleeping last night, I was planning for you, sir. Now I was taking a nap."

What Sherman planned was to press all along the line, at the same time sending one of McPherson's divisions directly south to probe for a crossing of the Oostanaula River; having crossed, McPherson's troops would then attempt to cut the railroad.

On the Federal left, John Schofield's Army of the Ohio was assigned to pierce the Confederate defenses at the head of Camp Creek. Schofield, who had arrived from the frontier war in Missouri the previous winter to assume command of the army, was 32 years old and a former roommate of McPherson's at West Point. A physics professor at Washington University in St. Louis before the War, Schofield was short and plump and rather dowdy. But his men took a liking to him. "It's all right, boys," one private remarked to his comrades. "I like the way the old man chaws his tobacco."

Schofield's little army included many raw

Pushing southeastward, Sherman advanced along the Western & Atlantic line with three armies under James McPherson, George Thomas and John Schofield. Reluctant to challenge Johnston's Confederates in the tortuous mountain passes, the Union commander repeatedly tried to turn his foe's western flank. Johnston, however, shifted his three corps under John Bell Hood, William Hardee and Leonidas Polk to meet the flanking threats. Sharp clashes resulted — along Rocky Face Ridge on May 8, outside Resaca a week later, and near Dallas beginning on the 25th. Each time, the Confederates were forced to give ground.

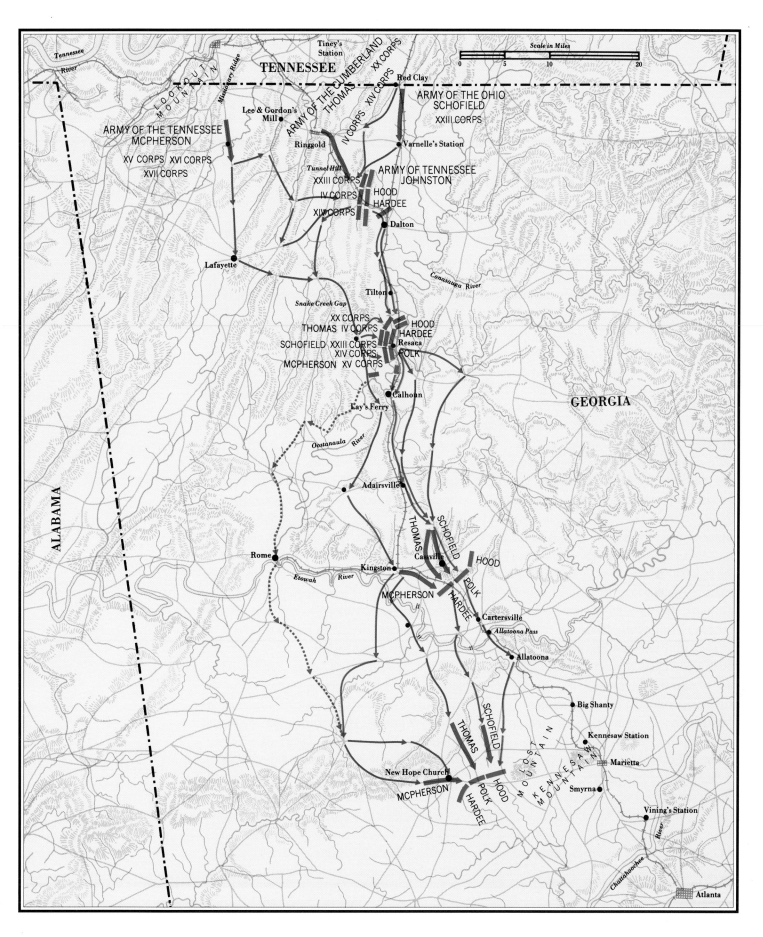

and undisciplined men from Kentucky and Tennessee. Its leadership also was largely unproved. Schofield, who himself was untried, fully trusted only one of his three division commanders, the capable Brigadier General Jacob D. Cox, and already had asked Sherman to replace Brigadier General Alvin P. Hovey, who he felt did not adequately respond to orders. Schofield also had doubts about his other division commander, Brigadier General Henry M. Judah.

Shortly after noon, Schofield launched two divisions abreast against Major General Thomas C. Hindman's Confederate division on the other side of Camp Creek; Cox attacked on the left and Judah on the right. "We charged across an open field interspersed with dead trees that flung out their ghostly arms to welcome us to the shadows of death," wrote Lieutenant John A. Joyce, adjutant of the 24th Kentucky. "A roaring fire of artillery burst from the enemy's works on the margin of the woods on our front; shot and shell fell among the dead tree-tops and crashed down upon the moving columns like a shower of meteoric stones."

Cox's division splashed across the shallow creek and captured part of Hindman's first line of entrenchments about 1:30 p.m. But within an hour, the attack foundered against stronger fortifications a few hundred yards farther ahead, costing Cox most of his day's toll of 562 casualties.

Meanwhile, on Cox's right, Judah's division fared even worse. First, Judah got his lines entangled with a division from the Army of the Cumberland that was meant to support him on the right. He did not halt to reorganize his confused men, nor did he wait for the supporting troops to get into position. In great haste, Judah ordered a charge across

Among the Federals to fall at Resaca on May 14 was Lieutenant Edgar J. Higby of the 33rd Ohio, killed during an assault on Confederate works. Described by a captain of the 33rd as a "brave and gallant youth," the 21-year-old Higby had recently rejoined his regiment after escaping from Richmond's infamous Libby Prison with 108 other officers in February.

the 400-yard-wide valley of Camp Creek.

This was open ground, and Hindman's defenders, concealed beyond the far bank of the creek, raked it with nearly continuous fire that cost Judah more than 600 men. Only a handful of Judah's troops got across the creek, and they had to seek shelter under its steep banks until darkness covered their withdrawal. For "incompetency displayed in handling his division" — some of his men thought he was drunk — Judah was soon relieved of his command.

While Schofield was being repulsed, Confederate scouts noticed an opening on the extreme Federal left. This position was occupied by Thomas' IV Corps, which had been posted at Rocky Face Ridge as a decoy. When the Confederates abandoned Dalton, the corps, under Major General Oliver O. Howard, had crossed Rocky Face and followed the enemy south. Facing south, most of Howard's troops had crowded right to link up with Schofield, leaving a division under Brigadier General David S. Stanley exposed on the left near the railroad.

About 4 p.m., the Confederates took ad-

On the Federal left at Resaca, the 5th Indiana Battery under Captain Peter Simonson fires on Hood's Confederates as Colonel James Robinson's brigade *(right)* provides support. In the close-quarter fighting that followed, Federals captured the flag of the 38th Alabama *(inset)*, inscribed with the names of some of the regiment's earlier actions in Tennessee and Georgia.

vantage of this gap. Two of John Bell Hood's divisions — strengthened by four brigades taken from the center and left of the Confederate line — slammed into Stanley's right flank. It was "a grand charge," wrote Thomas Deavenport, one of Hood's regimental chaplains, "and the enemy were driven hastily back from their entrenched position, leaving knapsacks, haversacks, guns."

The sudden attack stampeded Stanley's 35th Indiana, leaving only a battery of artillery — the 5th Indiana — to try to plug the hole. Firing double-shotted canister from the crest of a knoll, the Indiana gunners gouged big gaps in the gray lines. But the

Confederates pressed ahead on both sides of the knoll, threatening to envelop the guns.

Only the timely arrival of Federal reinforcements prevented a breakthrough. Major General Alpheus Williams' division marched at the double-quick over from the Army of the Cumberland in the center of the Federal line to rescue the threatened battery. Under withering new fire, the Confederate attack slowed, then receded around the base of the knoll. The Federal artillery was safe, at least for the time being.

Hood tried to regroup for another attack, but night fell and the fighting ended. Nevertheless, General Johnston was so pleased with Hood's initial success that he ordered him to renew the advance at dawn. Johnston hoped that Hood could turn the enemy left flank, then smash through to Snake Creek Gap, cut off the Federals from their supply wagons and sever their line of retreat.

The day's events had left Johnston in high spirits—but not for long. That night ominous reports reached the general from his left flank. First, he learned that, during the evening, part of McPherson's army had shifted south and without opposition had quietly oc-

cupied a hill that commanded Johnston's line of retreat from Resaca. Artillery on this hill would be capable of knocking out the railroad bridge and another span across the Oostanaula just south of town.

Then, about 8 p.m., came alarming news from scouts that a Federal division had crossed the Oostanaula at Lay's Ferry, six miles southwest of Resaca. The report was true enough—but misleading all the same.

In reality, General McPherson, following Sherman's orders, had dispatched a division

Brigadier General John K. Jackson (*mounted, at center*) launches a Confederate attack in the face of savage artillery fire near Lay's Ferry on the evening of May 15. Jackson's assault was part of the belated effort by division commander William Walker to dislodge Thomas Sweeny's Federals from their bridgehead south of the Oostanaula River.

under Brigadier General Thomas Sweeny southward to get across the river and into the Confederate rear.

Sweeny, a 43-year-old, one-armed Irishman who, according to a subordinate, spoke three languages — "English, Irish-American and profane" — had executed his mission well enough at the start that afternoon. He ordered most of his division to demonstrate on the north bank of the river at Lay's Ferry for the benefit of some Confederate cavalrymen on the south bank. Then, about 5 p.m., Sweeny launched some troops of the 81st Ohio and the 66th Illinois in five pontoon boats farther downstream. With about 20 men to the boat, the soldiers rowed across the river under a spattering of enemy fire and "with a bound and a yell and a volley," wrote one of the Ohioans, established a bridgehead on the south bank.

They were scarcely across, however, when

Sweeny received reports — erroneous, as it turned out — that a large Confederate force was crossing the river above Lay's Ferry. Fearing that his division would be cut off, he called back the boats and withdrew.

Up in Resaca that night, Johnston knew only that the Federals had reached the south bank. Faced by this apparent danger to the south and by the threat of Federal artillery to his bridges just below Resaca, he issued a series of orders to prepare for the worst.

Johnston called off the scheduled attack by Hood north of Resaca. He ordered immediate construction of a pontoon bridge a mile upstream from Resaca, beyond the reach of McPherson's guns. And he directed the division of Major General William H. T. Walker, which was posted a few miles south of Resaca, to march westward toward Lay's Ferry in hopes of heading off Sweeny's Federals at the Oostanaula.

Sherman was also busily making plans for the next day, Sunday, May 15. He ordered Sweeny's division, reinforced by a division of cavalry, to return to the Oostanaula and cross it again. And he called for a major push in the left center of the line, northwest of Resaca, near the mouth of Camp Creek, where Schofield's little Army of the Ohio had failed to make headway on Saturday.

In the morning, Schofield moved around to the extreme Federal left to make room for Major General Joseph Hooker's XX Corps of the Army of the Cumberland. Hooker, the well-known "Fighting Joe" who had once led the Army of the Potomac, would make the attack supported by Howard's IV Corps.

Just before noon, Hooker's troops moved out to the east on a three-division front roughly parallel with the Dalton-Resaca road. The road ran between a series of north-south ridges, and the ridge just east of it was occupied by one of Hood's divisions under Major General Carter L. Stevenson.

At the angle where Stevenson's line bent to the east, a point about three miles north of Resaca, a spur jutted westward from the ridge. In an unfinished earthen fort on this heavily wooded knob, Captain Max Van Den Corput had emplaced his Georgia battery of four 12-pounder Napoleons. The fort stood about 80 yards in front of the Confederate main line in a commanding position where the guns could enfilade advancing Federals. Infantrymen with spades were still working to finish the fort when Hooker's marching troops reached the next ridge to the west.

Sizing up the situation, Hooker instructed Major General Daniel Butterfield to take his division to seize the Confederate earthworks. His orders set in motion a furious little struggle during which, for those involved, the fate of the entire battle seemed to hinge on the control of those four guns.

Butterfield's 1st Brigade, under Brigadier General William T. Ward, spearheaded the attack in column of regiments. In the lead was the 70th Indiana, 400 men who, despite nearly two years of service, had never been under fire. These Hoosiers were commanded by Colonel Benjamin Harrison, the 30-year-old grandson of the ninth U.S. President, William Henry Harrison, and himself destined for the presidency.

Harrison led his troops down the slope and into the open valley that separated the two ridges, waving his cap and shouting, "Cheer, men, for Indiana! Forward! Double quick, march!" The Hoosiers surged ahead, maintaining their lines in parade-ground order despite galling fire from the fort and

from riflemen entrenched on the ridge. "They did not mind shot any more than a duck would water," wrote Van Den Corput, the battery captain.

The Hoosiers crossed the road and started up the wooded knob. Near the top, emerging from the dense underbrush, they ran into a wall of lead. The Georgia gunners were firing canister, discharging their pieces virtually into the faces of the Federals — "so close to us as to blow the hats off our heads," wrote one of the Hoosiers, Private William Sharpe.

The Federals flopped to the ground, seeking shelter behind the earthen parapets of the fort's outer ring, less than 10 yards away. Then Harrison, noticing that the Confederate infantry supporting the guns had fled to the rear, stood up and brandished his sword in one hand and his pistol in the other. With a yell, the Hoosiers swarmed into the fort.

In the melee that followed, a few of the gunners fled or took refuge beneath their gun carriages. But most of them defiantly stuck by their guns. Several artillerymen lashed out with their ramrods and were bayoneted in return. Others fought with clubbed muskets and their fists.

"One brave fellow would neither run nor surrender," recalled Captain William M. Meredith of the 70th Indiana, "but stood there laying about him with his ramrod. I had fired the last two shots of my revolver at him and had begged him to surrender, but his only reply was a swinging sweep of his ramrod. Then a hand reached over my shoulder, somebody said, 'Captain, let me at him,' a pistol was fired close beside me, and turning I saw Colonel Merrill, smoking revolver in hand."

More Federal regiments rushed into the fort and the issue was quickly settled. Of the

On May 15, men of Hooker's corps haul a Napoleon cannon from the captured Georgia battery as infantrymen duel with Confederates in the distance. Federals who had felt the force of the battery during the day were relieved to see the guns at last in friendly hands. Recalled a Wisconsin man: "That 4-gun battery was playing on us as fast as it could fire, and did some frightfully wicked work."

27 Georgians manning the guns, only five managed to escape. The others died or surrendered. One cannoneer tried to surrender, but someone noticed the words stitched on his coat sleeve — "Fort Pillow." Enraged by this reference to the Tennessee post where Federal soldiers, black and white alike, had been massacred the previous month, men of the 105th Illinois proceeded to shoot and bayonet the Confederate to death.

The Federals had captured the fort, but their position was untenable. The fort was exposed to fire from the Confederate main line and was the target of angry gunners elsewhere. By now Harrison was leading the brigade, having replaced Ward, who had been wounded in the fighting. Harrison pulled the regiments back to the shelter of the fort's western parapets. His Hoosiers and rem-

nants from other regiments in the brigade remained there all afternoon.

The four guns stood silent in the open fort between the lines, surrounded by dead men in blue and gray, until after dark. Then some Federals dug away part of the parapet, attached the guns to ropes and hauled them down the slope.

Later, several different Federal regiments would claim credit for having retrieved the guns, which in the memory of the claimants would shine as gleaming bronze. John Bell Hood, who lost them, remembered them differently — "four old iron pieces, not worth the sacrifice of the life of even one man."

The fight for the guns tended to overshadow more significant events taking place that Sunday afternoon. While Hooker's advance bogged down, the Battle of Resaca was being settled elsewhere in rather routine fashion.

Down at Lay's Ferry, Thomas Sweeny got his boats across the Oostanaula River. His division then laid a pontoon bridge and began erecting earthworks on the south bank. William Walker's Confederates arrived that evening—too late. They failed to dislodge the Federals, who, when reinforced the next morning, would be in a position to strike eastward at the rail line south of Resaca.

Once again, as at Dalton, Johnston had been outflanked and would have to pull back. At dark, he began the retreat from Resaca, using all three bridges over the Oostanaula. Fearing that Union artillery might begin shelling the two bridges within its range, the Confederates took pains to cover the noise of withdrawal. Pickets stayed in the lines and made a racket with rifle fire; artillerists laid green cornstalks over the bridges to muffle the rumble of gun carriages.

By dawn Monday, all Johnston's men were safely across the bridges and the general could rest easier. In the fighting at Resaca, he had suffered moderate casualties—about 2,600 killed, wounded or captured. The Federals lost 3,500. "We have had a heap of hard fighten," W. A. Stephens of the 47th Alabama wrote to his sister, "and have lost a heap of men and kild a heap of Yankes."

For the next two days, Johnston followed the railroad south, while to the rear Wheeler's cavalry kept up a running skirmish with Sherman's swiftly pursuing Federals. Unlike the rugged terrain around Resaca, the region south of the Oostanaula was gently rolling and mostly open country, and Johnston could not immediately find a suitable place to take a stand.

But on the night of Tuesday the 17th, at Adairsville, about 15 miles south of Resaca, Johnston happened upon some intriguing topography—a fork in the road leading south. The main road veered southeast to Cassville, a small college town 12 miles distant. The other road followed the railroad 10 miles south to Kingston before bending eastward to Cassville.

Johnston thought Cassville might be a good place to stage an ambush. He would send two thirds of his army, the corps of Polk and Hood, directly there. His third corps, under Hardee, would attempt to confuse the enemy by taking the road to Kingston.

Sherman, Johnston reasoned, would come to the fork at Adairsville and divide his army, taking both roads. Meanwhile, Hardee would hurry east from Kingston to join the rest of the army at Cassville. There, the reunited Confederates would overwhelm the isolated wing of the enemy.

On Wednesday, May 18, the Confederates carried out the planned movements from Adairsville. The Federals reacted just as Johnston had hoped. Confronted by the two choices at the Adairsville road fork, Sherman sent most of Thomas' troops to Kingston and Schofield's little Army of the Ohio, augmented by Hooker's corps, to Cassville. McPherson's army, in the meantime, was marching south on a track about five miles west of Adairsville. One Federal division, that of Brigadier General Jefferson C. Davis, was even farther extended: It followed the Oostanaula down to Rome, about 15 miles west of Kingston, and occupied that armaments center with only minor opposition on Wednesday.

On Thursday morning, May 19, Johnston prepared to spring his trap at Cassville. For once, his army would enjoy numerical supe-

Major General Thomas C. Hindman, whose Confederate division mounted a spirited defense at Resaca, was a onetime U.S. Congressman from Arkansas renowned for his fire-eating oratory. A Northern Congressman wrote, "It seemed as if he was perpetually anxious to have a duel." Wounded at Shiloh and at Kennesaw Mountain in June 1864, Hindman survived the War, only to be killed by an unknown assailant in 1868.

riority. The rest of Polk's troops from Mississippi had arrived, passing through Rome just before the Federals got there, and Johnston now had nearly 74,000 men. About two thirds of these troops were at Cassville, and Hardee was hurrying there from Kingston with the remaining corps. By contrast, the Federal wing now approaching Cassville under Schofield and Hooker consisted of fewer than 35,000 men.

Johnston was so confident he began the day by issuing a ringing proclamation to the troops. The weary days of retreat were over, he announced: "I lead you to battle." Cheers greeted Johnston's brave words as they were read to each regiment. "I never saw troops happier or more certain of success," a private recalled. "A sort of halo illuminated every soldier's face. We were going to whip and rout the Yankees."

This was to be accomplished from front and flank. To meet the Federal advance head on, Polk's corps was deployed across the Adairsville road northwest of Cassville. About a mile to Polk's right, meanwhile, Hood's corps was to march north on a parallel road, then turn west and fall upon the left flank of the advancing Federals.

But as Hood moved into position at mid-

morning, chance intervened. A detachment of Union cavalry had wandered several miles east, off the main line of Hooker's march, and wound up on Hood's right. An aide reported this unexpected presence to Hood, who realized that the Federals would be behind him if he faced west according to plan.

When word of this new development reached Johnston, he refused to believe it. His scouts had reported no such body of Federals. Years later, in fact, he insisted that it had not existed and that Hood had bungled a great opportunity. All the same, without sending an aide forward to verify the report, Johnston called off Hood's attack.

Johnston still hoped to salvage a victory at Cassville. He pulled back Hood and Polk and put them on a wooded ridge, just southeast of town, where they were joined late in the afternoon by Hardee's corps coming in from Kingston. The ridge, 140 feet high and more than two miles long, commanded the open valley in which the town lay. Johnston later remembered the position "as the best that I saw occupied during the war."

But late in the afternoon, part of his new line came under fire from Federal artillery as Sherman, rushing up from Kingston, began massing his forces just north and west of Cassville. The Federal guns, situated on a ridge less than a mile west of the Confederates, laid a punishing enfilade fire on the right center of Johnston's line.

Hood and Polk met that night with Johnston and insisted that this enfilade by enemy artillery would make it impossible for them to hold their ground.

What they advised Johnston to do became another of the many controversies in the acrimonious postwar dispute that developed between Hood and Johnston. Hood wrote after the War that he and Polk wanted to launch an attack from the ridge. Johnston said the two favored retreat. He agreed, he said, because their lack of confidence in the position "would inevitably be communicated to their troops" and thus be self-fulfilling.

A day that had begun with stirring hopes of victory ended with the bitter taste of another retreat — "a step which I have regretted ever since," Johnston wrote. At midnight the Confederates started south again, following the railroad nine miles to Cartersville. There, on May 20, they crossed the Etowah River and continued a few miles farther, taking up positions around Allatoona Pass, where the railroad crossed the 1,000-foot-high Allatoona Mountains.

Sherman had fully expected to fight on Friday the 20th and was surprised to find Johnston gone again. He did not immediately pursue the Confederates across the Etowah but paused "to replenish and fit up." Colonel William W. Wright's 2,000-man Railroad Construction Corps had rebuilt the burned bridge at Resaca in only three days, and on Friday the first supply trains arrived at Kingston. "Locomotives whistled merrily right up to our camps," wrote one Federal.

Sherman wrote his wife, Ellen, noting with pride that his campaign thus far had been "rapid, skillful and successful." In just two weeks his armies had covered more than half the distance to Atlanta.

When he resumed the advance, Sherman intended to keep on flanking. From his days as an artillery lieutenant in the region 20 years before, he was aware of the natural strength of Johnston's new position at Allatoona Pass. ("I knew more of Georgia than the rebels did," he bragged after the War.)

The pass was stronger than the "terrible door of death" at Rocky Face Ridge.

Sherman decided to skirt the pass to the south by cutting loose from the railroad. He would load his wagons with 20 days' supplies and march to a little crossroads town named Dallas, 22 miles south of his present field headquarters at Kingston and about 15 miles southwest of Allatoona Pass. Then, having outflanked the Confederates and forced them to abandon their mountain stronghold, he intended to head east to rejoin the railroad at Marietta.

On Monday, May 23, Sherman rode south with his three armies across the Etowah, which he confidently called "the Rubicon of Georgia." Only one more river, the Chattahoochee, six miles from Atlanta, stood between him and the Gate City. "We are now all in motion like a vast hive of bees," he wired his chief quartermaster back in Nashville, "and expect to swarm along the Chattahoochee in five days."

But it would not be that easy. So rough was the broken and unmapped terrain beyond the Etowah — "very obscure," Sherman noted, "densely wooded and with few roads" — that it took two of those days just to get within striking distance of Dallas. And on Wednesday morning, May 25, when Hooker's corps reached Dallas in the lead, an unpleasant surprise was waiting.

As usual, Joseph Johnston had exercised what Sherman later referred to as his "lynx-eyed watchfulness." Alerted at Allatoona by his cavalry that Sherman was up to his old flanking tricks, Johnston had responded by sidestepping in a southwesterly direction with his entire army. His new line occupied some low wooded ridges, extending from a mile south of Dallas to a crossroads about

Federal troops perched on boxcars arrive from the north at the Georgia town of Kingston as wagons assemble alongside in this sketch by artist J.F.E. Hillen. At Kingston, several miles above the Confederate stronghold at Allatoona Pass, Sherman left the rail line, sending his men and wagons south on a flanking course.

four miles northeast of town at a Methodist meetinghouse called New Hope Church.

Around 10 a.m. on Wednesday, Joseph Hooker's leading division, under Brigadier General John Geary, was advancing southeast on a road that led to New Hope Church when it encountered two regiments of Alabama and Louisiana men. Geary drove the Confederates back but learned from prisoners that Hood's entire corps was entrenched near the church a couple of miles down the road. Geary went as far as a ridge opposite the one occupied by Hood, then halted to pile up log breastworks and wait for reinforcements.

Sherman rode over to the sound of the fir-ing and ordered Hooker to attack. He waited with mounting impatience while Hooker brought up his two other divisions, which had been heading for Dallas on separate roads several miles apart. Sherman, who did not like Hooker anyway, doubted the reports that Hood's whole force was already entrenched at the church. "I don't see what they are waiting for in front now," Sherman growled to a staff officer. "There haven't been 20 rebels there today."

It was after 4 p.m. and dark thunderclouds were rolling in from the southwest when Hooker at last launched his attack. Geary's troops were in the middle, flanked on the right by Daniel Butterfield's division and on the left by that of Brigadier General Alpheus S. Williams.

Williams, a 53-year-old veteran known to his men as "Pop," was grinding away on an unlit cigar — a sure sign he expected a big fight. Moving forward through the dense underbrush of blackjack bushes, Williams got his men across the valley and to the foot of the enemy ridge.

Then, about 50 yards from the Confederate main line, the division was forced to halt in the face of what Williams called the "most effective and murderous fire." It seemed to him that it came from "all directions except the rear." In no more than 20 minutes, Williams later reported, 745 of about 7,500 men fell dead or wounded.

Geary and Butterfield were also having a hard time — partly because of the manner in which Hooker had deployed his corps. Because of the dense forest on his flanks, Hooker ordered that each division advance in a column of brigades, one brigade behind another. But this formation exposed masses of men behind the front rank to fire that they could not return for fear of hitting their comrades. It also meant that the entire front of Hooker's attacking force, which consisted of nearly 20,000 men, was only three brigades wide — about the same width as the Confederate division directly confronting them.

That Confederate division, occupying the center of Hood's line near the church, was commanded by Major General Alexander P. Stewart. A West Pointer and former mathematics professor, Stewart was a 42-year-old veteran of all the battles fought by the Army of Tennessee and was much admired by his men, who knew him as a strict disciplinarian and referred to him as "Old Straight."

To support his three infantry brigades, Stewart had massed in his front line three batteries of artillery. These 16 guns were able to concentrate their fire with devastating effect against the narrow front of the Federal advance. In less than three hours, the cannon unleashed into the tightly packed Federal ranks no fewer than 1,560 rounds of shell and canister.

But the Confederate batteries also suffered dearly because of their exposed position in the front line. Forty-four horses were hit, and 43 men were killed or wounded. Among the casualties were three courageous brothers in Captain Charles E. Fenner's Louisiana Battery. "The oldest was a rammer," wrote one of Stewart's aides, Lieutenant Bromfield L. Ridley. "He was shot down and the second brother took his place. In a short time he too was shot down and the third brother took his place when shortly he was shot, but stood there until a comrade came to relieve him."

At the peak of the fighting, a courier rode up to Stewart with a message from the commanding general. Stewart was facing odds of more than 3 to 1 while Confederate divisions on either side of his position were practically idle. Johnston wanted to know if he needed help. "My own troops will hold the position," replied Old Straight.

About 7 p.m., the darkening sky finally erupted. Thunder and lightning outmatched the roar and flash of Stewart's guns. Then came torrents of rain that literally drowned out the Battle of New Hope Church. As the firing subsided, Rice C. Bull of the 123rd New York heard one of his comrades, lying in a pool of water, jokingly offer to "swim over and tackle the Johnnies."

In Hooker's corps, 1,665 soldiers were killed or wounded that day; Hood lost not quite half that many men.

The rest of the Federal army came up during the night and on Thursday morning, May 26, sloshed through the mud to take up positions parallel to the six-mile-long Confederate line. The nature of the terrain and Sherman's own inclinations meant that there would be no large-scale attack. The loblolly pines grew "almost as closely as a canebrake," wrote Jacob Cox, and were "nearly impenetrable for man or horse."

Sherman, having failed in the assault at New Hope Church and finding no apparent weakness elsewhere during probes on Thursday, decided to seek out the enemy's far-right flank and attempt to turn it. On Friday morning, he sent a force of about 14,000 Federals under the IV Corps commander, Oliver Howard, toward a grist mill known as Pickett's Mill, about two miles northeast of New Hope Church.

It was hard going, "through dense forests and the thickest jungle," reported one of Howard's division commanders, Brigadier General Thomas J. Wood. He and Howard kept peering through their field glasses in search of the entrenchments on the enemy's extreme right. Finally, about 2:30 that afternoon, Howard concluded he had located the

A view of the field at New Hope Church after the battle on May 25 shows Confederate breastworks, fashioned of dirt packed around a frame of timbers. General Alexander Stewart, who led the defenders, remarked that two of his brigades "had piled up a few logs." But to the Federals, the fire from such impromptu barriers proved devastating.

end of the enemy line near Pickett's Mill.

He deployed his forces to attack in a southeasterly direction. Brigadier General Richard W. Johnson's division from the XIV Corps was to support the attack on the Federal left, and a brigade from the Army of the Ohio was to shield the right. Wood's division was to spearhead the assault with the 1,500-man brigade of Brigadier General William B. Hazen in the lead.

Hazen was 33, a veteran general who was quick to attack the enemy and just as eager to get embroiled in disputes with his superiors. "A synonym of insubordination," a fellow brigadier said of him. "The best-hated man that I knew," remarked the writer Ambrose Bierce, who served him as a topographic officer, "a skillful soldier, a faithful friend and one of the most exasperating of men."

Hazen said nothing at the time, but he must have fumed inwardly at the clumsy Federal preparations. Howard had brought no artillery. He had worn out his men thrashing awkwardly through the woods looking for the Confederate flank. And now he took two full hours to form for the attack in a column of brigades, the same narrow deployment that Hooker had unwisely used at New Hope Church two days before.

Howard was not at all sure of himself that afternoon, and his uncertainty was revealed in a short note he sent his army commander, George Thomas, at 4:35 p.m. "I am now turning the enemy's right flank," said Howard, "I think."

In fact, Howard had not reached the Confederate flank. What he had perceived as the end of the enemy line was merely a slight bend in it. The flank extended beyond Howard's left and was covered by several hundred of Brigadier General John P. Kelly's dismounted Confederate cavalrymen. And in front of Howard waited nearly 4,700 infantrymen of Patrick Cleburne's division — regarded as the best in the Army of Tennessee — who had been moved there the previous day to extend Hood's right.

Cleburne knew the attack was coming. A reconnaissance by Brigadier General Daniel C. Govan's brigade had spotted the Federal movement that morning and had followed it by the sound of bugle calls and of blueclad hordes thrashing about in the thickets.

At 5 p.m., Hazen began his advance and almost immediately ran into Confederate skirmishers on his left — Kelly's dismounted cavalrymen firing their carbines from behind heaps of little stones they had piled up. Pushing on, Hazen crossed a wide ravine and climbed a long slope studded with rock outcroppings. Deployed at the top under their distinctive blue battle flags were Cleburne's three brigades: Govan's Arkansas troops, Brigadier General Hiram B. Granbury's Texans and a brigade of Alabamians under Brigadier General Mark P. Lowrey.

Part of the Confederate line was protected by rifle pits and log revetments, but some grayclads lay prone, protected only by rocks or folds in the ground. Hazen's men, seeing their enemy without fortifications, sprang forward shouting. "Ah, damn you," a Federal soldier yelled. "We have caught you without your logs now!"

Cleburne's men, whose training had always emphasized rapid-fire marksmanship, opened up at point-blank range. Their fire was augmented from the Confederate left by a pair of howitzers from Captain Thomas J. Key's Arkansas Battery, which caught Hazen's right in a murderous stream of case shot and canister.

Men of the 78th Pennsylvania doffed their hats for this group portrait atop Lookout Mountain before marching into Georgia. Caught in the open at Pickett's Mill on May 27, the Pennsylvanians held for four hours, fighting with what their brigade commander termed a "persistency and heroism worthy of all praise." The regiment suffered 49 casualties before being ordered to withdraw.

Hazen got within 20 paces of Granbury's line on the Confederate right, but no farther. Blueclad bodies began to pile up. In a matter of 45 minutes, Hazen estimated, his brigade lost 500 men killed or wounded.

Then, with their ammunition depleted, his men broke and scurried toward the ravine about 80 yards behind them. As they regrouped in the rear, Hazen later wrote, his men were in "bad humor." They grumbled that they had been "sold out" — not properly supported — by Johnson's division on the left, which was held back by the Confederate cavalrymen, and by the brigade on the right, which failed to come up.

Even worse, General Howard committed Wood's two other brigades with agonizing slowness — at 40-minute intervals, reported Hazen. In any case, Hazen's men were already spent when the next brigade came up.

This new wave of Federals, under Colonel William H. Gibson, marched against Cleburne's wall of fire with even higher casualties and no better results — but not for lack of trying. The color-bearer of the 15th Ohio, Sergeant Ambrose D. Norton, struggled to within 15 paces of the Confederate line, planted the regimental flag, and then fell dead. Ohioan after Ohioan — five in all — attempted to recover the flag, and each was felled before Sergeant David D. Hart brought it safely back. Another of Gibson's regiments, the 49th Ohio, sent more than 400 men into the battle and lost 203 of them. "This is surely not war," a Federal wrote later; "it is butchery."

Shortly before dark, as Confederate artillery shells endangered the Federal rear, Howard sent in Wood's remaining brigade just to hold the line. A shell fragment already had put one Union general, Richard John-

son, out of action with a severe wound in the side. Now, as Wood's last brigade started forward, a shell exploded near Howard.

Howard, who had suffered the loss of his right arm two years before at Fair Oaks, Virginia, felt the impact and thought for a moment he had lost a leg. But when he summoned the courage to look down, he saw that a fragment of the shell had merely ripped off the heel of his boot.

The firing gradually subsided after sundown. Over in the Confederate line, however, Granbury's Texans noted with distaste that a number of Federals still held out in the ravine in front of them. These Federals were "moving among the dead leaves on the ground," wrote Captain Samuel T. Foster of the 24th Texas Cavalry (Dismounted), "like hogs rooting for acorns."

At 10 p.m., with their bayonets fixed, the Texans rushed down into the pitch-black ravine — "yelling like all the devils from the lower regions had been turned loose," said Foster. They captured 232 Federals, about a third of whom were wounded.

All told, more than 1,600 Federals were lost in Howard's abortive assault, whereas Confederate casualties numbered no more than 500. After the War, Ambrose Bierce wrote that the Federal attack belonged to that class of events "foredoomed to oblivion" — officially forgotten by General Sherman, who omitted all mention of Pickett's Mill in both his official report and his voluminous personal memoirs.

Sherman's ill-fated foray led Joseph Johnston to suspect that the Federals, by extending to their left, might be weakening their right. Accordingly, the following day, Saturday, May 28, he ordered Hardee to probe in

Brigadier General Hiram Granbury, in civilian dress for this 1862 portrait, led the fierce nighttime charge of the Texas Brigade that ended the Battle of Pickett's Mill. "It needed but the brilliancy of this night attack," Confederate commander Patrick Cleburne wrote, "to add lustre to the achievements of Granbury and his brigade."

force to test the defenses of McPherson's army, which was south of Dallas. The assignment fell to the division of Major General William B. Bate, which held the extreme left of the Confederate line.

Bate's plan was to lead off on his left with a brigade of dismounted cavalry under Brigadier General Frank C. Armstrong. If Armstrong found the Federal trenches abandoned, as suspected, he was to fire four cannon shots as a signal to Bate's infantry, which would then attack.

About 3:45 that afternoon, Armstrong's cavalry stormed out of the brush "with a yell the devil ought to copyright," as a Federal later wrote. The Confederates hit the Federal right flank just south of Dallas and found McPherson's XV Corps well entrenched. But the surprise and momentum of the attack carried Armstrong's men past the first line of fortifications, where they overran three exposed guns of the 1st Iowa Battery.

The XV Corps commander, Major General John Logan, rushed to the front, "growling at the situation," as an observer put it. Known to his troops as "Black Jack" for his swarthy complexion, dark hair and sweeping mustache, Logan was an Illinois politician and one of the best of the politically appointed Union generals, though the West Pointers tended to distrust his flair for the dramatic. Even in battle, General Stanley noted acidly, "Logan always played to the gallery."

At the front, Logan found disorganized groups of Federals milling around asking for their regiments and officers. Waving his sword, Logan shouted, "Damn your regiments! Damn your officers! Forward and yell like hell!" With the men rallying behind him, he jumped his horse over some earthworks and headed for the cannon the Confederates had seized. A bullet hit him in the left forearm, but Logan improvised a sling and stayed in the saddle while his men recaptured the guns.

Meanwhile, over in the Confederate line, Bate's infantry heard the firing and mistook it for the signal to attack. Soon after 4 p.m. Bate's Florida Brigade and, to its right, the 1st Kentucky Brigade surged forward against the heavily fortified lines of the Federal XV Corps and of the XVI Corps farther north. They emerged from the underbrush to encounter what one Confederate described as "a sheet of flame."

The Florida Brigade suffered heavy casualties and soon fell back under orders. But word of its retreat failed to reach Brigadier General Joseph H. Lewis' 1st Kentucky, the veteran outfit widely known as the Orphan Brigade. Many of the Orphans were proudly wearing new uniforms issued that day. They swarmed over the first line of Federal

Rallying his men with a wave of his hat, Major General John (Black Jack) Logan rides forward to counter the threat to the Federal right at Dallas on the afternoon of May 28. A contemporary likened Logan to an Indian chief for his dark complexion and implacable demeanor.

works and then, without support on either flank, slugged it out with the main line only 50 yards away.

The Orphans found cover behind logs, abandoned haversacks and even their own dead. One regiment, the 5th Kentucky, worked its way to within 20 yards of the Federal works and stayed there resolutely behind any protection the men could find.

As the firing intensified, soldiers of the 5th Kentucky fought with uncommon valor, none more so than an enlisted man named James Cleveland. At the height of the battle, bullets kept finding Cleveland with tragic accuracy. One struck his left arm and another hit his chest, but Cleveland fought on. Then, in quick succession, a ball went through his bowels, another smashed the elbow of his other arm and yet another bruised his face. Only then, wounded five times, did Cleveland give in. And yet somehow he had the strength to crawl back to the Confederate lines and cling to life for a week before death claimed his riddled body. When the brigade finally got the order to retire, the 5th Kentucky refused to budge. Only when the regi-

mental commander, Lieutenant Colonel Hiram Hawkins, seized the colors and waved them frantically did these men fall back.

The Orphan Brigade contributed heavily to the Confederate losses of more than 700 that afternoon. By one account, the Orphans lost 51 percent of the men engaged in a battle that lasted no more than an hour.

Despite that defeat, the Confederates continued to attack, and they kept McPherson pinned down through the waning days of May. Then, on June 1, his Army of the Tennessee finally managed to disengage and — entrenching and fighting as it moved — to follow the two other Federal armies in a slow and intricate sidestep to the left.

On that same day, Sherman sent Brigadier General Kenner Garrard's division of cavalry north to occupy the now lightly defended Confederate stronghold at Allatoona Pass. He was moving his armies back to the railroad, abandoning his former plan of flanking the enemy on the south.

Instead of swarming across the Chattahoochee, Sherman's armies had gotten bogged down fighting what he called "a big Indian war" in which every tree and log seemed to shelter an enemy sharpshooter. His Army of the Cumberland alone was expending 200,000 rounds of ammunition every day with little gain.

Sherman wanted out and so did his soldiers, who were sick of the heat, the stench of unburied bodies, and the incessant skirmishing and sharpshooting. For years they would remember that arduous last week in May not in terms of the three major engagements — New Hope Church, Pickett's Mill and Dallas — but as one endless battle. They referred to it all simply as the "Hell Hole."

Standoff at Kennesaw Mountain

"The wonder was that any lived through such a storm of shot and shell and grape and canister and musket balls. It was a costly experiment, and, judged by the event, without a single, actual, compensating return."

MAJOR JAMES T. HOLMES, 52ND OHIO, AT KENNESAW MOUNTAIN

During the first week in June, the opposing armies took up new positions astride the railroad that sustained them. On June 3 the first of Sherman's Federals, sidestepping northeastward from Dallas, arrived at the little rail town of Ackworth. On the following night, Johnston's Confederates, realizing the threat to their right flank, abandoned Dallas in a torrential rain and entrenched on a new line intersecting the Western & Atlantic about eight miles below Ackworth.

Sherman was now "in the very heart of Dixie," as one of his officers put it in a letter home. He was 12 miles north of Marietta, the rail town he originally had hoped to reach in his aborted flanking maneuver via Dallas, and only about 30 miles from Atlanta itself.

Out on the new Federal picket line, a soldier from the 104th Illinois called to his Confederate counterpart: "Hello, Johnny, how far is it to Atlanta?"

"So damn far you'll never get there."

"Yes, we *will* get there, and we'll have a big dance with your sister!" With that, a shower of Confederate bullets put an end to the conversation.

In order to reach Atlanta, the Federals had to pass through rough terrain studded with four mountains. Three of these mountains defined the new 10-mile-long Confederate line, which extended across the railroad on a southwesterly axis. Brush Mountain, just north of the Western & Atlantic, anchored the line on the Confederate right, and Lost Mountain the left. In the middle, Pine Mountain jutted slightly forward, bowing the line toward the Federals.

The fourth mountain stood about two miles in the rear of the new line and gave the Confederate position its greatest strength. A humpbacked ridge two miles long, Kennesaw Mountain rose nearly 700 feet above the rugged landscape. Already bristling with cannon, the mountain's defenses watched over the railroad, which skirted the base of its towering northern peak. Kennesaw also shielded Johnston's new headquarters at Marietta and blocked the way to the Chattahoochee, the last broad river remaining in Sherman's path. As Sherman described the mountain in a dispatch to Washington, "Kennesaw is the key to the whole country."

By June 11, Sherman had his armies moving again. He now mustered more than 100,000 men, approximately the strength with which he had started five weeks before.

His battle losses of 9,209 men during May had been nearly replaced by the 9,000 troops of XVII Corps, newly arrived from Northern furlough, under Major General Francis Preston Blair. This former Congressman and brother of Lincoln's Postmaster General also brought with him several hogsheads of ice and numerous baskets of champagne. (Joseph Johnston, lacking the luxury of either champagne or reserve manpower, was unable to replace all 8,500 troops lost to combat in May; his army now numbered fewer than 70,000 men.)

This straw hat, a relic of Joseph E. Johnston's Confederate army, was worn during the Atlanta Campaign by James J. Lampton, an enlisted man in the 13th Mississippi; Lampton was killed in the fighting in July 1864. The hat had been lovingly woven for him by his sister, Josephine.

Deployed on a 10-mile front, the Federals moved forward slowly, feeling for the enemy main line, which intersected the railroad a couple of miles below the town of Big Shanty. On the Federal left, McPherson's Army of the Tennessee headed down the railroad toward Brush Mountain; on the right, Schofield's Army of the Ohio moved toward Lost Mountain; and in the center, Thomas' Army of the Cumberland approached the most vulnerable part of the enemy's line — the salient jutting forward at Pine Mountain.

By Monday, June 13, Thomas had worked two of his corps around the base of the mountain toward the east. This maneuver threatened to isolate one of William Hardee's Confederate divisions, which was posted on the mountain. Growing concerned about the danger, Hardee asked Johnston to examine the position with him.

On the morning of June 14 the two commanders, along with the bishop-general Leonidas Polk, rode to the crest. They dismounted and, attracting a cluster of soldiers, climbed on an artillery redoubt to survey the Federal forces spread out on the plain 300 feet below.

Less than a half mile away, inspecting his own line, stood General Sherman. He looked up at the group of grayclad men on the mountaintop. He did not know who the Confederates were, but their presence irritated him. "How saucy they are!" he exclaimed, and ordered a few rounds of artillery fire to "make 'em take cover."

The order went down the line to an Ohio battery commanded by Captain Hubert Dil-ger. A former officer in the army of the German Grand Duchy of Baden, Dilger was one of the best-known artillerists in the Federal Army. He habitually wore an immaculate white shirt with sleeves rolled up and doeskin trousers, which were the source of his nickname "Leatherbreeches."

Dilger showed flair as well in his strange manner of giving commands: He had trained his artillerymen to respond to carefully rehearsed claps of his hands. The crews followed his cues with such speed and precision that Dilger's superiors let him place his battery wherever he wished. That position was usually so near the front that one general jokingly offered to equip Dilger's cannon with bayonets.

Dilger sighted in the target on Pine Mountain. He clapped his hands, the guns roared and the first salvo landed close enough to startle the Confederate generals. Johnston and Hardee ran for cover. The portly Polk, his hands clasped behind his back in an apparent attempt to maintain dignity in the presence of the troops, moved less quickly.

Another clap of Dilger's hands sent more rounds crashing into the mountaintop. One of the shells hit Polk in the left arm, tore through his body and emerged from his right side before exploding against a tree. The bishop-general died instantly. As Polk fell, Johnston braved another salvo and rushed forward, cradling him in his arms. In Polk's jacket pocket, now soaked with blood, were three copies of a little book of religious inspiration entitled *Balm for the Weary and Wounded*. Polk had inscribed the books with Johnston's name and Hardee's and Hood's, intending them as gifts.

A wave of anguish ran through the Army of Tennessee. Polk had been with it since before Shiloh and was the army's most beloved general. Though scarcely a military genius — "as a soldier he was more theoretical than practical," wrote one of his division commanders — Polk had served as a kind of spiritual beacon for generals and privates alike. That night, before the Confederates abandoned the mountain stained with his blood, someone chalked a message on the door of a log cabin: "You damned Yankees, you have killed our old General Polk."

To Sherman, who learned of the death when a signalman intercepted a Confederate semaphore message requesting an ambulance for Polk's body, the event was scarcely remarkable. On both flanks, as well as in the center, his armies were forcing the outmanned Confederates to pull back and contract their overextended line. On the evening of the 15th he wired Washington, "We killed Bishop Polk yesterday, and have made good progress today."

During the following days, however, Sherman had to measure his advance in yards rather than in miles. His success thus far had been based on maneuver so skillful that even his enemy expressed grudging admiration. "Sherman'll never go to hell," said a captured Confederate. "He will flank the devil and make heaven in spite of the guards."

But now, rapid movement was impossible. One reason was the rain. It poured down incessantly, turning the roads into what one Confederate called "liquid mud." "Rain! Rain! Rain!" wrote J. L. Ketcham of the 70th Indiana. "I never saw the like." Some soldiers swore that it was brought on by the continuous roar of artillery and musketry.

Sherman's progress was hindered as well by the tendencies toward trench warfare

evidenced earlier at Dallas and New Hope Church. Now, the attackers as well as the defenders were taking the time to entrench at every opportunity.

The Federals had to do most of their own digging, although Sherman did authorize each division commander to hire up to 200 freedmen as $10-a-month laborers to work at night while the soldiers slept. The Confederates, by contrast, often were able to retreat into elaborate breastworks already prepared by slaves. "The whole country is one vast fort," Sherman wired Washington, "and Johnston must have at least fifty miles of trenches with abatis and finished batteries."

Even the skirmishers on both sides dug in. And it was here, on the skirmish line, that most of the fighting raged as the Federal trenches inched toward Kennesaw. "The skirmish is kept up night and day," wrote Robert Patrick, a Confederate supply clerk, "and the work of death goes on the while, like the current of the flowing river, slow and even sometimes, and at others as rapid as a cataract."

The "work of death" was about to accelerate. The Confederates, falling back gradually, relinquished all of their high ground except massive Kennesaw Mountain. On June 19 they forged a new and stronger line about five miles long. Centered on Kennesaw's slopes, it extended north across the railroad and south to a knoll two miles below the mountain.

Sherman responded by extending his right farther to the southeast. This movement, although slowed by the continuing rain, threatened to flank the mountain and cut the railroad as it swung south out of Marietta two miles behind Kennesaw.

Slow to follow Generals Hardee and Johnston (*foreground*) toward cover during a burst of artillery fire, General Leonidas Polk is killed instantly by a direct hit from a Federal shell on June 14, 1864. "The death of this eminent Christian and soldier," Johnston later wrote, was the result of Polk's "characteristic insensibility to danger."

Johnston countered by extending his own left flank. On June 20 he replaced Hood's corps on his extreme right with Joseph Wheeler's cavalry division; Johnston then sent Hood marching south behind Kennesaw Mountain to take up a new position on the extreme Confederate left. On Wednesday, June 22, Hood deployed his three divisions across the Powder Springs road near a plantation called Kolb's farm, about three miles southwest of Marietta.

It was the first day of sunshine in at least a week, and in front of Hood the Federal right wing was taking advantage of the dry weather. The Federals were advancing east toward Kolb's farm astride the same Powder Springs road — Joseph Hooker's XX Corps on the left of the road and a division of Schofield's Army of the Ohio on the right of it.

Around noon, Federal skirmishers captured several prisoners and learned from them some alarming news: Hood planned to attack. Indeed, skirmishers from the 123rd New York were able to creep close enough to Hood's lines in the woods to hear the preparations for the assault.

Why Hood wanted to attack is a mystery. Perhaps he thought his position lay beyond the Federal right and he would be able to flank the enemy. Yet he seems neither to have carefully scouted the terrain in front of him nor to have ascertained the strength of the Federals he would fight. What is certain is that Hood decided on his own: He did not bother to consult his commanding general, Joseph Johnston.

Late that afternoon, two of Hood's divisions emerged from the woods on both sides of the road. The division of Carter Stevenson led the assault, supported on his right by that of Thomas Hindman. Their path led almost due west across the partly cultivated fields of Kolb's farm and across a pair of parallel ravines cut by small streams.

About a half mile away, deployed on a series of ridges, the Federals waited. Alpheus Williams' division occupied the center. On his right, across the road, was Schofield's division under Brigadier General Milo Hascall. On Williams' left, separated from him for several hundred yards by a creek and swampy ravine, stood John Geary's division.

Having been forewarned by their skirmishers, the Federals dug in as best they could and piled up barricades of logs and fence rails. Their line covered at least a mile and a half and contained nearly 40 cannon. They outnumbered the attackers by about 14,000 to 11,000.

Stevenson's infantrymen, arrayed elbow-to-elbow in three lines of battle, headed directly toward Williams' sector of the line. Williams scrambled atop a pile of fence rails to get a better view. From this exposed position, he began directing his artillery fire. The first shells hit the closely packed Confederate ranks at a distance of about 500 yards.

Federal guns joined in all along the line. They fired shell and solid shot first, then switched to case and canister as the Confederates kept coming. Together the guns were pumping out iron at the rate of 90 rounds a minute. The Confederates who managed to survive this maelstrom swore afterward they had never endured heavier fire, not even in the far-bigger battles at Chickamauga and at Missionary Ridge.

Wide gaps opened in Stevenson's lines, but his assault surged down into the ravine nearest the Federals and then up the slope. His men were now within 200 yards of the Federal line, charging into point-blank fire from artillery and muskets. To make matters even worse, the Confederates were now caught in their left flank by canister from Hascall's 19th Ohio Battery, which was posted just beyond the road.

The canister roared out of the guns "like a tornado," wrote one of the Ohio gunners, T. C. Tracie. "Volley after volley was sent plunging and tearing through the massed lines, strewing the ground with fallen men."

Stevenson's assault came within 50 yards of Williams' line, and then it broke. His men withdrew to the ravine to regroup. They mounted a new charge, fell back and then, gallantly and without gain, charged again.

On Stevenson's right, the attack led by Hindman also faltered. His men lagged behind Stevenson's and got bogged down in the swampy bottoms of the westerly flowing creek that separated the Federal divisions of Williams and Geary; then they were caught in a withering enfilade on their right from Geary's batteries.

Hindman's men retreated to the woods. Stevenson's battered troops hung on in the shelter of the ravine in front of Williams, listening in the gathering dusk to the Federals taunting them to try another charge.

During the night, the Confederates made their way back to the woods in small groups, carrying their wounded with them. The next day, a Northern newspaper correspondent inspected what they had left behind. The stream in the ravine, he wrote, was "choked up with bodies and discolored with blood."

Hood's ill-considered assault cost him nearly 1,000 men, 870 of them from Stevenson's division. Johnston did not learn of these losses from Hood, however. Having neglected to tell his commanding officer about the attack beforehand, Hood also failed to report to him the full dimensions of the disaster — an oversight that would fuel the postwar feud between the two men.

On the Union side, the commander in chief turned out to be less than happy with his own corps commander, Joseph Hooker. Though Hooker's hard-fighting XX Corps was responsible for the victory, and at a loss of fewer than 300 men, Sherman chose to find fault with a message Hooker had sent him during the attack. Sherman professed to be angry because Hooker's message exaggerated the size of the enemy force and ex-

Federal fieldpieces blast away at Kennesaw Mountain on June 27 in an attempt to soften Confederate breastworks built as high as seven feet and as thick as nine feet. The bombardment did little damage to such fortifications, but its intensity impressed the Confederate defenders. "Hell has broke loose in Georgia, sure enough!" one of them exclaimed.

Kennesaw's Bombardment

MAP ON OTHE SIDE —

6u

pressed undue concern for his right flank, which was secure.

These points were so trivial that Sherman obviously had seized upon them to try to cut his ambitious subordinate down to size. Hooker had a reputation for exploiting political influence to snipe at his superiors behind their backs.

So, on the day after the Battle of Kolb's Farm, Sherman delivered a stern lecture to Hooker about the excesses of his battlefield message. "I reproved him more gently than the occasion demanded," Sherman wrote in his memoirs, "and from that time he began to sulk."

Sherman's irritation widened during the next few days as the fighting subsided to the frustrating rhythm of trench warfare. The presence of Hood on the Federal right prevented the intended flanking maneuver there. And Sherman could not extend farther to the south beyond Hood until the roads dried and ensured the necessary flow of supply wagons that far from the railroad.

The mountain itself, together with the foothills extending below it, stymied Sherman's left and center. Confederate fortifications covered the western slopes of the mountain's prominences, which descended like tree-carpeted stairsteps to the south: first, the highest peak at 700 feet, which was known as Big Kennesaw; then the 400-foot Little Kennesaw; finally, the 200-foot-high knob called Pigeon Hill, where great flocks of passenger pigeons roosted during their annual migration.

The Federals brought their own trenches to a perimeter several hundred yards from the base of the mountain but were unable to get any nearer. Sherman tried pummeling the mountain with artillery. He ordered up 140 field guns, and the word went through the Federal trenches that "Old Billy" was determined to take Kennesaw "or shoot it damn full of old iron."

After the shellfire proved ineffective, Sherman determined to take the mountain by assault. On June 24 Sherman told his commanders to get ready to attack the Kennesaw line in three days. His plan was based on his assumption that the enemy had weakened its defenses in the middle in order to strengthen the flanks. While the Federal troops demonstrated all along the line, two major assault columns would hit the Confederates where Sherman figured they least expected it — in Johnston's right center, near the south end of the mountain, and in his center, a mile below the mountain. If these attacks succeeded, reinforcements would follow, driving through to the railroad and splitting the Confederate army in two.

Sherman's principal subordinates, recalling the heavy losses incurred in the head-on assaults around Dallas the previous month, showed little enthusiasm for the plan. According to XV Corps commander John Logan, James McPherson quietly suggested that it might be more prudent to wait until the roads dried and then outflank the enemy. Sherman replied, said Logan, that "it was necessary to show that his men could fight as well as Grant's." As the troops made preparations, they too regarded the prospect of a head-on attack with grave doubts. Men in one of George Thomas' regiments, the 34th Illinois, were taking bets that they would never get past the Confederate skirmish line.

On Monday, June 27, the day of the battle, "the sun rose clear and cloudless," wrote a Confederate soldier. "The heavens seemed made of brass and the earth of iron, and as the sun began to mount toward the zenith, everything became quiet and no sound was heard save a peckerwood on a neighboring tree, tapping on its old trunk, trying to find a worm for his dinner."

At 8 a.m., the silence of the Kennesaw line was shattered by the roar of more than 200 Federal cannon. From the mountain came the Confederate artillery's full-throated reply. "Gun spoke to gun," wrote Lieutenant Colonel Joseph S. Fullerton, a Federal staff officer. "Kennesaw smoked and blazed with fire, a volcano as grand as Etna."

On the brow of Little Kennesaw, where his men had dragged nine guns, Confederate Major General Samuel French was "enjoying a bird's eye view." He watched while "as if by magic, there sprang from the earth a host of men, and in one long, waving line of blue the infantry advanced."

Along most of the curving, eight-mile front, Federal skirmishers were moving for-

Starting out at 8:30 a.m. on June 27, more than 13,000 Federal infantrymen assaulted Confederate-held Kennesaw Mountain: On the left, Morgan Smith's division from the Army of the Tennessee led the attack against Confederates commanded by Samuel French and William Walker. On the right, two divisions from the Army of the Cumberland led by Jefferson Davis and John Newton assaulted a salient — later called the Dead Angle — defended by two Confederate divisions under Benjamin F. Cheatham and Patrick Cleburne. Both thrusts were halted with heavy losses. Meanwhile, John Schofield's Army of the Ohio pressed forward on the Confederate far left in an advance that turned into a full-scale flanking movement.

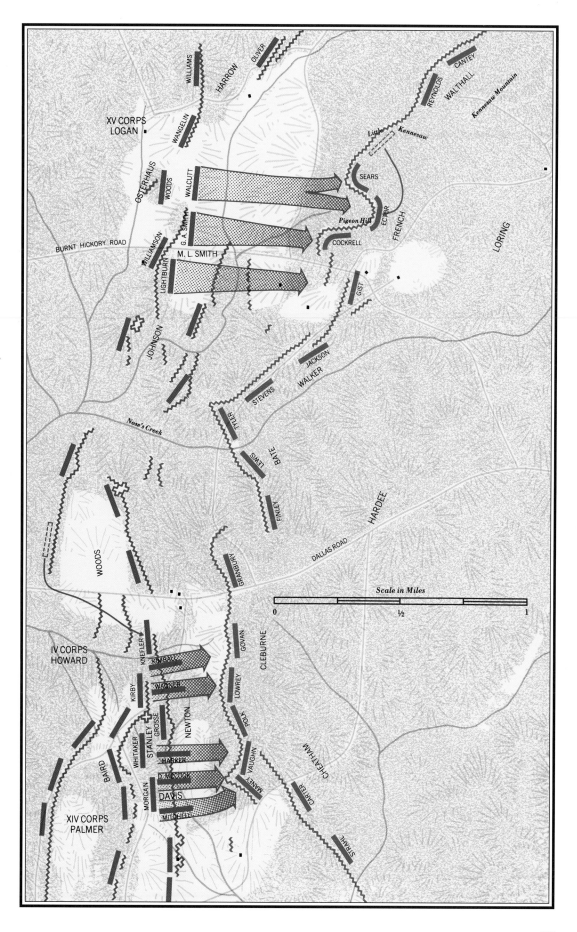

67

ward. But French and the other Confederate commanders quickly saw that much of this was feint. They directed their artillery fire instead on the blueclads emerging from the woods in force: a single division near the southwest slope of Little Kennesaw, and two divisions south of the mountain complex itself. Soon the sharp crack of musketry, combined with the sound of French's own guns, produced what he called "a roar as constant as Niagara."

It fell to McPherson's Army of the Tennessee to make the assault on the Confederate right center. About 8:30 a.m., after the artillery duel had ceased, three brigades under Brigadier General Morgan L. Smith moved east toward the southern slope of Little Kennesaw and the spur just below, Pigeon Hill. They deployed on a half-mile front astride the Burnt Hickory road, 5,500 men in two columns of regiments facing 5,000 entrenched Confederates.

As soon as the Federals crossed a swamp, they encountered enemy troops in two lines of rifle pits. To Smith's right, the Federals were met by the 1st and 63rd Georgia Regiments of General William Walker's division. Though greatly outnumbered here, the defenders put up a fight.

The Georgians resisted with clubbed muskets and anything else within reach. In one rifle pit, 11 Georgians battled hand-to-hand until nine of them were bayoneted. In another pit, Lieutenant George A. Bailie, his ear grazed by a bullet, saw his Federal assailant standing 20 feet away, reloading to fire again. Bailie, armed only with a sword, picked up a stone and hurled it directly between the eyes of the Federal, knocking the soldier to the ground.

Nearby, a little Georgia Irishman by the name of John Smith wrestled with a Federal for control of his own musket — and lost. Shoving his opponent backward, Smith shouted, "To hell with you and the gun, too!" and ran to the rear.

The Federals soon overran the pits, capturing or disabling more than 100 men. Then they started up the steep slope of Little Ken-

Resplendent on a black charger, Major General John A. Logan (*left, center*) watches as troops of his Federal XV Corps advance toward the smoke-wreathed, Confederate-held heights beyond. Logan's objective was to drive a wedge between Little Kennesaw (*background, left*) and a nearby knob called Pigeon Hill, thereby splitting the Confederate line.

quickly faltered. As the Federals struggled through and over these obstacles, they ran into musket fire from the front and a vicious enfilade from French's batteries posted on Little Kennesaw. "Within about thirty feet of the enemy's main works," reported the Federal division commander Morgan Smith, "the line staggered and sought cover as best they could behind logs and rocks."

Before the bugle sounded retreat, Smith had lost 500 of his men, including seven regimental commanders. Then, shortly before 10 a.m., his brigades withdrew to the rifle pits they had overrun an hour before and took refuge there.

A mile and a half to the south, meanwhile, below the mountain itself, the other major Federal assault was developing. At 9 a.m., two divisions from Thomas' Army of the Cumberland, having formed south of the Dallas road, moved forward against the center of the Kennesaw line. The attack matched 8,000 Federals against an equal number of Confederates who were defending a long ridge.

The two Federal divisions advanced simultaneously — John Newton's IV Corps division on the left, Jefferson Davis' of the XIV Corps on the right. According to Thomas' orders, the five attacking brigades advanced in close-packed columns rather than in broad lines of battle. The columnar formation, what one officer called "a human battering ram," enhanced the chances of piercing the enemy line. But it also provided a massed target for the enemy and tended to break down quickly if the leading regiments did not keep moving.

On Newton's right, the advance became confused almost as soon as it got under way.

nesaw on the left and the lesser incline of Pigeon Hill on the right. The main Confederate line stretched out above them about 500 yards distant.

But the intervening ground was strewn with so many obstacles — felled timber, boulders and the spiked logs called chevaux-de-frise — that the momentum of the charge

This right-flank brigade was commanded by Brigadier General Charles G. Harker, who at 27 was one of the most promising field officers in the Union Army. A West Pointer, he had already distinguished himself at Stones River and Chickamauga, and he was still lame from a wound received at Rocky Face Ridge. "Anything that required pluck and energy," said his corps commander, Oliver Howard, "we called on Harker."

But on this day luck deserted Harker. His tight column of five regiments broke up as the men scrambled over their chest-high entrenchments and struggled through the abatis that lined their works. Instead of charging in a solid block, they neared the Confederate earthworks in a trickle of desperate men.

Then Harker's attack collapsed in the murderous fire from Brigadier General Alfred Vaughan's Tennessee brigade. Those Federals who were not killed or wounded huddled on the slope in front of the Confederate works. "Occasionally some gallant soldier would rise up with a stand of colors in his hand," wrote Lieutenant John Shellenberger of the 64th Ohio. "The movement would begin to spread, when a volley would come from the works, cutting down the leaders, and the movement would then subside."

One of the few Federals to reach the objective was Michael Delaney, color-bearer for the 27th Illinois. Delaney drew his revolver and leaped onto the parapet. For a moment, the Stars and Stripes floated above his en-

While the Battle of Kennesaw Mountain continues to rage in the background, men of the 1st and 15th Arkansas (*left*) observe a short-lived truce, watching as Federal troops carry their wounded from the path of a rampaging brush fire. Standing on the parapet is Colonel William H. Martin, the Confederate who called the truce; he was severely wounded shortly afterward.

70

emy. Then Patrick Cleburne's men descended on Delaney from both sides and jabbed him with their bayonets. Still clutching the flag, he staggered back, mortally wounded and crying in vain to his comrades, "Boys, save the colors!"

Harker, determined to renew the assault, galloped up the slope, waving his hat and shouting, "Come on, boys!" Harker and his staff rode along the Federal lines within 15 yards of the blazing Confederate defenses. Just as the general reached the 42nd Illinois, a bullet tore through his right arm and into his chest. Harker toppled from his horse, and now his men retreated down the corpse-strewn slope, bearing their commander with them. Later General Sherman would write, "Had General Harker lived I believe we would have carried the parapet, broken the enemy's center, and driven him pell-mell into the Chattahoochee."

Nearer the Dallas road, Newton's other two brigades had also struggled without gain. In front of the Confederate section held by one of Cleburne's Arkansas regiments, scores of Federal wounded lay unattended between the lines.

Now these helpless men faced a new danger. Gunfire had ignited the underbrush and flames were flashing through the woods, roasting some of the wounded alive and threatening to reach still others.

Watching in horror from the Confederate entrenchments, Lieutenant Colonel William H. Martin, commander of the consolidated 1st and 15th Arkansas, ordered his regiment to cease firing. He tied his handkerchief to a ramrod and jumped onto the parapet to offer a truce. "Come and remove your wounded; they are burning to death," Martin shouted to the Federals. "We won't fire a

gun until you get them away. Be quick."

Then, while gunfire continued to roar along the rest of the line, a merciful quiet settled over this little part of the mountain. Men in blue from Illinois came out from behind boulders and fallen trees; men in gray and butternut from Arkansas clambered over their parapets. Working together, they carried the wounded men to safety in the Federal rear.

After the charred area was cleared and the flames were stamped out, a Federal major approached Martin and presented tokens of appreciation: a pair of matched Colt revolvers. On that note, the truce ended and the men who had shared an extraordinary act of kindness went back to their savage war.

In a short time, however, Newton's three brigades — having suffered in less than two hours most of their 654 casualties for the day — fell back and dug in. In places the lines were only 40 yards apart.

Beyond Newton's right, meanwhile, the battle had reached a crescendo with the advance of the two brigades under Jefferson Davis. Here, at a point one half mile south of the Dallas road and two miles below the mountain, was "the storm center," wrote Colonel James Nisbet of the 21st Georgia — the scene of what he described as "the most desperate fighting of the war."

Davis' objective was a knoll defended by two entrenched brigades under Major General Benjamin Franklin Cheatham, a hard-drinking, 43-year-old veteran.

Cheatham's line jutted forward on the hill and then cut back toward the east to form a sharp-angled salient. In his honor the knoll would later be named Cheatham Hill. And for the many who died there that Monday morning, the salient would be known thereafter as "the Dead Angle."

Davis' advance began on a sober note. One of his brigade commanders, Colonel Daniel McCook Jr., walked along the lines of anxious men reciting a poem by Thomas Macaulay; the verse depicted the legendary Roman warrior Horatius as he faced battle in defense of a bridge over the Tiber:

> *Then out spake brave Horatius,*
> *The Captain of the Gate:*
> *To every man upon this earth*
> *Death cometh soon or late,*
> *And how can man die better*
> *Than facing fearful odds,*
> *For the ashes of his fathers*
> *And the temples of his gods.*

The blueclads listened carefully: Their young commander was one of the famous Fighting McCooks — 17 brothers and first cousins in Federal blue, three of whom already had died for the Union.

Unlike Horatius' men, McCook's brigade was not outnumbered. The "fearful odds" that McCook contemplated were those presented by the perilous nature of the impending advance: covering 600 yards of rocky ground and a timber-covered slope to reach an open field that was commanded by Confederate fortifications.

And on McCook's right, in Colonel John Mitchell's brigade, the men of the 34th Illinois were also worried. They were the ones who had been taking bets that their advance would get stalled in front of the entrenched Confederate skirmish line partway up the hill.

But the Illinoisans surprised themselves. They deployed as skirmishers in front of the other five regiments of Mitchell's brigade, raced ahead and swept over the first Confederate rifle pits with ease.

The charge up Cheatham Hill — toward the southern flank of the Dead Angle — was a different matter. Mitchell's men felt spent even before they emerged into the open field near the enemy works. Their advance had begun at too fast a pace, and the midmorning heat — the temperature had reached almost 100° — had sapped their energy.

A storm of missiles spewed from the Confederate works: bullets and canister, entrenching tools, stones and even clods of dirt. A stone knocked off the cap of one Illinois soldier and then a 20-pound boulder slammed into his midsection, shoving him back down the slope. Soon all of Mitchell's regiments were pinned down in front of the Confederate breastworks. The commander of the 98th Ohio later wrote, "It was almost sure death to take your face out of the dust."

While Mitchell's assault sputtered and stalled, Fighting Dan McCook's column — just to the north — pressed on toward the point of the Dead Angle. To Lieutenant Frank B. James of the 52nd Ohio, "the air seemed filled with bullets, giving one the sensation experienced when moving swiftly against a heavy wind and sleet storm." Private Cyrus Fox of the 86th Illinois saw trees "torn into basket shives" by the bullets and shells; "it did not appear that a bird could have gone through there without being torn in small bits."

Up ahead, from the shelter of the Confederate breastworks, Sam Watkins of the 1st Tennessee contributed more than his share of bullets. His musket became so hot, he remembered, "that frequently the powder would flash before I could ram home the ball." He switched rifles with disabled com-

Confederate leaders in the bloody salient called the "Dead Angle" were Brigadier Generals Alfred Vaughan (*left*) and George Maney (*right*). Both officers survived the battle unscathed, but Vaughan had a leg blown off a week later at Vining's Station; he used the crutch that he holds in the picture for the rest of his life.

At the height of the struggle for the Dead Angle, a Confederate volley staggers the enemy attackers in a drawing done later by a Confederate soldier who fought there. The Confederate trenches seemed "veritable volcanoes," wrote one Union veteran, "vomiting forth fire and smoke."

rades and kept firing — 120 rounds in all.

At the same time, 10 Confederate cannon posted to the left and right of the Dead Angle kept up a terrible enfilade of shell and canister. Through the crossfire McCook's narrow column struggled, advancing to within 20 yards of the Confederate line. "They seemed," wrote the Confederate Watkins, "to walk up and take death as coolly as if they were automatic or wooden men."

Making a suicidal dash, McCook himself reached the Confederate lines, with a handful of men following. He scrambled on top of the parapet, and shouting, "Surrender, you traitors!" he slashed at the defenders with his sword.

In desperation, Private S. M. Canterbury of the 86th Illinois grabbed at McCook's coattails, saying, "Colonel Dan, for God's sake get down, they will shoot you."

"God damn you," McCook replied. "Attend to your own business."

Seconds later a Confederate thrust his musket against McCook's chest and pulled the trigger. Fatally wounded, the colonel fell backward off the works and was carried to the rear, gasping, "Stick to them, boys!"

After McCook was felled, his brigade inspector, Captain William W. Fellows shouted, "Come on, boys; we'll take . . ." A volley cut short his exhortation, and he fell dead. Colonel Oscar F. Harmon of the 125th Illinois was the next to take command of the brigade; in less than five minutes a bullet passed through his heart.

Nowhere at the Dead Angle were Davis' brigades able to sustain their assault. "It became," one Federal later wrote, "a slaughter of men like beasts in the shambles." The combined toll of Davis' casualties for the day amounted to 824; in McCook's brigade alone the casualty rate reached 35 percent.

Orders came to retire. Few men went far. It was safer to dig in than to retreat. Scarcely 40 yards from the tip of the dreaded Dead Angle, survivors of McCook's brigade improvised a line sheltered by a rise in the ground, scooping out shallow trenches in the hard red clay with bayonet and tin cup.

By noon it was clear to Sherman, watching from his headquarters on Signal Hill, a mile or so to the rear, that the assault had failed everywhere. Smith, Newton and Davis could all hold their ground but no more than that. Sherman also had reports of the appalling casualties that, when the final count was in, would mount to nearly 3,000 — compared with no more than one fourth that among the Confederates.

Even so, he could not let go. Twice that afternoon Sherman queried Thomas about renewing the attack. In reply to the second message, the loyal and taciturn Thomas put it bluntly, "One or two more such assaults would use up this army."

But Sherman had grown hardened to the killing. "Our loss is small, compared with some of those East," he told Thomas. And in a letter to his wife a few days later he would confess: "I begin to regard the death and mangling of a couple thousand men as a small affair, a kind of morning dash."

As it was, by that evening Sherman had come to a startling conclusion about his current tactics. Reports from Schofield on the southern flank made Sherman realize he no longer had to batter his armies against the Kennesaw line. Schofield already had outflanked it. Even before the assault was launched that morning, Schofield — demonstrating in support of the main attacks — had

Three of the Fallen

DANIEL McCOOK JR.

CHARLES G. HARKER

OSCAR F. HARMON

Among the nearly 1,500 officers and men lost by General George Thomas' Army of the Cumberland in the futile Union attacks on the Kennesaw heights were the three promising young commanders shown above.

Youngest of the group was 28-year-old Charles G. Harker, a West Point graduate who had been promoted to the rank of brigadier general for leading units through such bloody battles as Stones River and Chickamauga. Colonel Daniel McCook Jr., 30 years old, was well known as one of 17 McCooks — brothers and cousins — to serve in the Federal forces; he was so beloved by his brigade that the survivors held special reunions in "Colonel Dan's" honor for decades after the War. Colonel Oscar F. Harmon, 37, a leading Illinois lawyer before the War, was remembered as having "the solicitude of a father for his regiment" in camp and "the courage of a lion" in battle.

moved two brigades across Olley's Creek a mile or so below the Powder Springs road. This gain, which Sherman would describe as "the only advantage of the day," put Schofield beyond Hood's extreme left.

Sherman's seemingly futile main assaults thus served an ironic end. By diverting the Confederates' attention from the south flank, the principal thrusts had inadvertently served as demonstrations that enabled Schofield to make his move.

Schofield's bridgehead on the south bank of Olley's Creek paved the way for a major flanking operation. Before undertaking it, however, Sherman had to wait until the roads baked hard enough to permit him to break loose from his rail supply line.

There was also grim business to attend to. By Wednesday, June 29 — two days after the battle — the stench of the dead lying between the lines had become so oppressive that both sides agreed to a seven-hour truce. Federal soldiers fashioned grappling hooks from bayonets and, with the help of the Confederates, dragged the bloated corpses into deep trenches for burial.

While this grisly work proceeded, the enemies took advantage of the truce to trade coffee and tobacco. Several Confederate officers mingled with blueclads; some of the Federals crowded admiringly around General Cheatham to get the autograph of the commander responsible for their bloody repulse at the Dead Angle.

On Saturday, July 2, Sherman judged the roads dry enough to begin the big move around the southern flank of the Kennesaw line. That night he pulled McPherson's Army of the Tennessee from his left and sent it marching south behind Thomas' front to reinforce Schofield on the right. Brigadier General Kenner Garrard's cavalry division took McPherson's place in the line.

Up on Kennesaw Mountain, the Confederates were also on the move that night. Once again, the cat-and-mouse game had begun. Anticipating Sherman's turning maneuver, Johnston evacuated the line he had held so effectively for two weeks and withdrew to previously prepared works on a ridge astride the railroad at Smyrna, four miles southeast of Marietta.

When Sherman found the Confederates gone early the next morning, he sent Thomas in quick pursuit through Marietta. Sherman himself rode into town, pausing there long enough to administer a sharp reproof to General Garrard, who had moved too cautiously to suit him.

Unaware of the strength of Johnston's new line at Smyrna, Sherman was confident that the Confederate commander would keep retreating until he crossed the Chattahoochee, 10 miles southeast of Marietta; and Sherman wanted to catch him in the confusion of crossing. After all, Sherman told Thomas that evening in a message revealing his respect for Johnston, "no general, such as he, would invite battle with the Chattahoochee behind him."

But Johnston surprised Sherman by standing fast and inviting battle at Smyrna the next day, July 4. Sherman declined the invitation. He used Thomas' army to skirmish in front while bringing up McPherson and Schofield on the extreme Confederate left. This flank was vulnerable, guarded only by cavalry and a division of 3,000 hastily trained young boys and old men belonging to the Georgia state militia, which had recently been called up by the Governor.

Johnston responded to the threat and abandoned Smyrna that night; but he fooled Sherman again by remaining north of the Chattahoochee. His army retreated six miles to the north bank of the Chattahoochee, where for the past two weeks more than 1,000 slaves had been building unusually formidable fortifications.

This new line was six miles long and a mile deep, permitting all the infantry and artillery to be concentrated. The cavalry was dispatched to the south bank to guard crossings up and down the river. The line itself covered the railroad bridge and three pontoon bridges, which would allow for a quick exit over the river.

The fortifications had been designed by Johnston's chief of artillery, Brigadier General Francis A. Shoup. In addition to the usual rifle pits, the works contained a series of redoubts made of logs and packed earth up to 12 feet thick. A stockade of vertical logs linked these redoubts, which stood about 80 feet apart. The intervals were studded with artillery batteries and with heavy siege guns brought up from Mobile.

Such was Johnston's confidence in the new line that he felt certain he could hold Sherman north of the Chattahoochee River "a long time."

Sherman, too, admired the Chattahoochee defenses. Riding down from Smyrna on the morning of July 5, he viewed the new Confederate line from a hill near Vining's Station about two miles from the river. He thought it

Company A, 52nd Ohio, musters for a photograph at their camp near McAfee's Church in northern Georgia in the early spring of 1864, before they joined the rest of the Army of the Cumberland on the march toward Atlanta. The 52nd Ohio formed part of Colonel Daniel McCook's brigade, which spearheaded the assault on the Dead Angle at Kennesaw Mountain.

"one of the strongest pieces of field fortification I ever saw."

But from the same hill Sherman glimpsed something that excited him more. With "his eyes sparkling and his face aglow," according to one witness, Sherman saw for the first time in his two-month-long campaign the ultimate objective: Atlanta, with its spires and rooftops beckoning from a distance of no more than eight miles.

The urge to smash through Johnston's line and march into the city must have been powerful. This time, however, Sherman exercised patience and skillful planning. He posted the armies of Thomas and McPherson in front of the Chattahoochee fortifications to preoccupy the Confederates. He also sent a division of cavalry downstream to mislead them into thinking he intended a crossing to the south.

But his real objective was to flank the Confederates from the north. Even as Sherman stood on the hill near Vining's Station, the cavalry division of Kenner Garrard — the general he had reprimanded two days before for excessive caution — was hurrying toward the town of Roswell, 20 miles upstream, under orders to secure the bridge there.

Garrard arrived in Roswell that day to find that the bridge had been destroyed. The town's textile factories were operating full tilt, however, turning out cotton and woolen cloth for Confederate uniforms. Garrard burned every one of them, even a factory that was flying the French flag in a feeble show of neutrality. Under Sherman's orders, Garrard arranged to send more than 400 employees — mostly women who had originally come from the North — to Marietta for rail transport to Indiana and safety.

While Garrard scouted for a suitable ford across the rain-swollen river, Sherman dispatched Schofield on a personal reconnaissance to find a closer crossing. On July 7 Schofield discovered a lightly guarded gap in the Confederate cavalry screen about eight miles upriver, where Soap Creek emptied into the Chattahoochee.

The following morning, the resourceful Schofield set about securing a bridgehead on the south bank near a Confederate cavalry outpost. He sent a detachment across on the piled-up rocks of a submerged fish dam situated a half mile above the mouth of Soap Creek; nearer the creek, he launched an assault party in 20 pontoon boats. The two groups then teamed up on the south bank of the Chattahoochee to scatter the Confederate troopers and capture their one cannon without sustaining a single casualty. Before midnight, Schofield had two pontoon bridges in place and an entire division across the river.

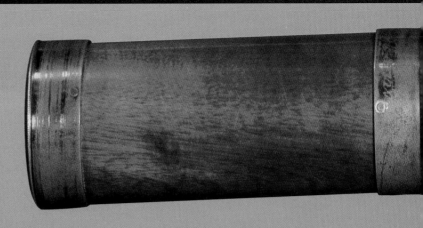

When Johnston was alerted on July 9 to the danger posed by Schofield's mile-deep bridgehead eight miles upriver, he was compelled to abandon his fortifications on the north bank. That night another enactment of the now-familiar rituals took place: the tramp across bridges strewn with green cornstalks to muffle the sounds of retreat, the burning of the railroad trestle, the dismantling of the pontoons.

By Sunday, July 10, Johnston's Army of Tennessee had left the Chattahoochee behind. Johnston marched the army a few miles east onto a ridge behind Peachtree Creek, a westward-flowing tributary of the river. This line, with the left extending across the railroad to the Chattahoochee, faced north to cover Atlanta, which was a mere five miles to the rear.

Sherman celebrated his latest achievement by taking a much-needed bath in the river. The following morning, July 11, he wired Washington, "We now commence the real game for Atlanta."

He spent the next six days moving everything into place. His armies built bridges, brought up supplies to a new rail depot at Vining's Station and expanded three bridgeheads—at Roswell, at Soap Creek and at a point just a couple of miles upriver from the abandoned enemy fortifications.

Meanwhile, the threat of Sherman's armies aroused near-panic among the citizens of Atlanta. Wagons crammed with the household effects of fleeing Atlantans crowded the streets. Frightened people jammed every train leaving town.

The alarm was nearly as great in Richmond. President Davis and his Cabinet, having fretted for two months as Johnston re-

Ambrose Bierce at War

"My duties as topographical engineer kept me working like a beaver—all day in the saddle and half the night at my drawing-table," recounted the narrator of a story written in the 1880s by Ambrose Bierce, one of America's foremost authors. Bierce's character was drawn from firsthand experience—having enlisted in the 9th Indiana at the age of 18, Bierce joined the staff of General William B. Hazen as acting topographical officer in 1863. Using the tools shown here, Bierce translated his observations of terrain into finished maps (*far right*). "It was hazardous work," explained Bierce's fictional counterpart. "The nearer to the enemy's lines I could penetrate, the more valuable were my field notes and the resulting maps. The lives of men counted as nothing against the chance of defining a road or sketching a bridge."

Throughout the Atlanta Campaign, Bierce's own daring forays nearly cost him his life. On June 23, 1864, in a skirmish at Kennesaw Mountain, Bierce was severely wounded and put out of action until after the fall of Atlanta.

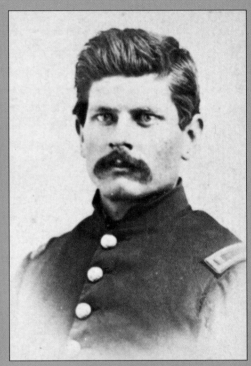

LIEUTENANT AMBROSE BIERCE

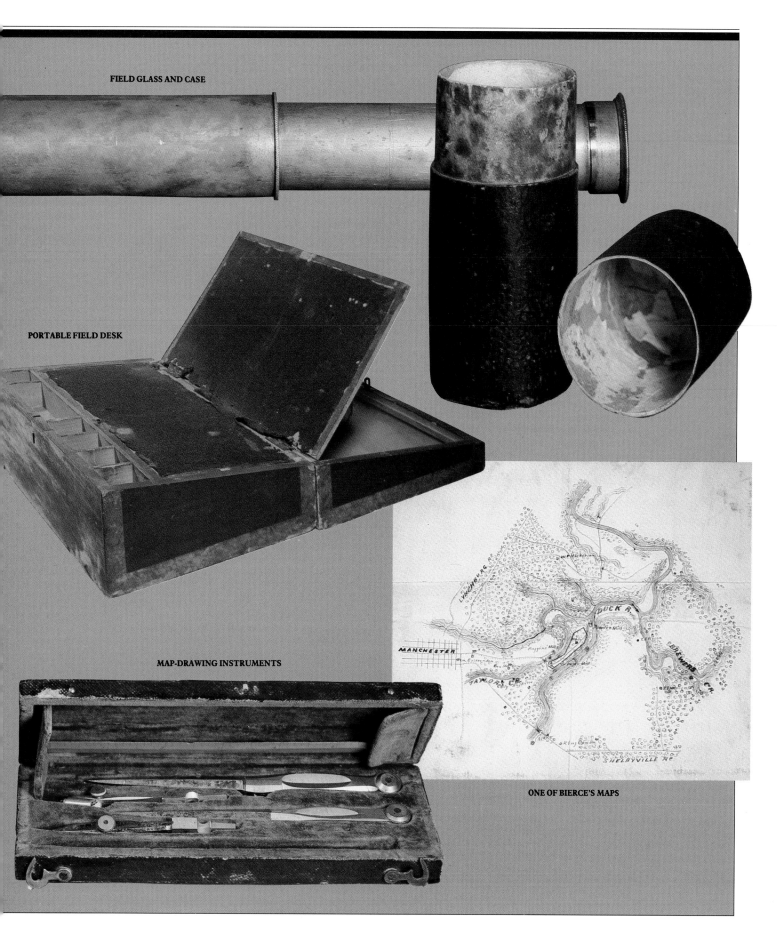

FIELD GLASS AND CASE

PORTABLE FIELD DESK

MAP-DRAWING INSTRUMENTS

ONE OF BIERCE'S MAPS

treated every step of the way from Dalton, now feared that he would fail to stand fast in front of Atlanta itself.

Such was the strain between Davis and Johnston that every communiqué from the field was scrutinized in Richmond for hidden meanings. On July 10, for example, Johnston sent a message recommending the immediate evacuation of the big prison camp at Andersonville, 125 miles south of Atlanta. Johnston's message was prompted by his concern that Sherman might send a flying column of cavalry to liberate the 30,000 Federals incarcerated there; Davis interpreted it as an indication that his general was about to abandon Atlanta.

Desperate to be apprised of Johnston's intentions, Davis dispatched to Atlanta a personal emissary, Braxton Bragg, the former commander of the Army of Tennessee and now the Confederate President's chief military adviser. The choice of Bragg for such a delicate mission was hardly politic, because Joseph Johnston held his predecessor and the President in equal scorn. Johnston had recently remarked of Davis: "He tried to do what God failed to do. He tried to make a soldier of Braxton Bragg, and you know the result. It couldn't be done."

Bragg, after his arrival in Atlanta on July 13, met several times with John Bell Hood, whose disparaging reports in the spring had helped discredit his commander in Richmond. Hood again shaded the facts, asserting that he had constantly urged Johnston to give battle and that Johnston had repeatedly missed opportunities to take the offensive. Bragg passed these damaging reports on to Richmond along with his own erroneous assessment that Johnston appeared ready to evacuate Atlanta.

Brigadier General Kenner Garrard incurred the wrath of General Sherman by not pursuing the retreating Confederates swiftly enough through Marietta: "Get out of here quick," Sherman yelled to him. "Go for the rebs." Garrard redeemed himself by forging a bridgehead on the Chattahoochee River beyond the Confederate flank.

In his talks with Johnston, Bragg concealed the purpose of his mission, insisting that the visit was unofficial. In any event, he apparently was able to learn little from Johnston. "He has not sought my advice and it was not volunteered," Bragg telegraphed the President on July 15. "I cannot learn that he has any more plans in the future than he has had in the past."

On the following day President Davis resorted to a blunt telegram to Johnston himself, demanding to know "your plan of operations so specifically as will enable me to anticipate events."

Much later Johnston would assert that he had had a plan in mind all along. According to his memoirs, he intended to wait for the Federal armies to become divided while crossing Peachtree Creek, then pounce on them separately.

But Johnston stubbornly refused to take the President into his confidence. Now, in reply to Davis' wire, he offered only vague

Following Garrard's cavalry, Major General Grenville Dodge's XVI Corps fords the Chattahoochee at Roswell's Ferry. Dodge's men had marched 31 miles from the Federal right flank to the extreme left, playing a key role in the deft maneuvers that forced the Confederates to abandon their defenses along the river.

generalities: "As the enemy has double our numbers we must be on the defensive. My plan of operations must, therefore, depend upon that of the enemy."

Sherman's advance on Atlanta began Sunday morning, July 17. All three Federal armies were now across the Chattahoochee, marching from their bridgeheads on an enormous wheeling maneuver designed to bear down upon the city from north and east.

That night, at the Confederate headquarters three miles northwest of Atlanta, Johnston conferred with his chief engineer about strengthening the city's fortifications to meet the Federal advance. At 10 p.m., the arrival of a telegram interrupted the meeting. It was from Richmond, from the Confederate Army's adjutant and inspector general, Samuel Cooper, who notified Johnston:

"I am directed by the Secretary of War to inform you that as you have failed to arrest the advance of the enemy to the vicinity of Atlanta, far in the interior of Georgia, and express no confidence that you can defeat or repel him, you are hereby relieved from command of the Army and Department of Tennessee, which you will immediately turn over to General Hood."

An Epic View of the Fight for Atlanta

Early in 1887, a mammoth circular painting called a cyclorama went on display in Detroit, the first stop on an exhibition tour of American cities. On a canvas 52 feet high and 377 feet in circumference, a team of German-born artists (*pages 88-89*) had rendered in near-photographic detail and with scrupulous accuracy the Battle of Atlanta, which raged east of the Georgia city on July 22, 1864.

Intent on depicting a decisive moment in the battle, the artists focused on the fighting between the Federal XV Corps and Major General Benjamin Cheatham's Con-

Firing from windows of the Troup Hurt house (*above*) and from behind an improvised barricade of logs and cotton bales, Alabamians under Brigadier General Arthur Manigault confront counterattacking Federals at a critical moment in the Battle of Atlanta. At left, soldiers of the 55th Illinois advance toward a cut on the Georgia Railroad, beyond which can be seen the church spires of the city. Near the railroad tracks are dead horses and wrecked limbers from Battery A, 1st Illinois Artillery, which had been overrun in the initial Confederate attack.

federate corps, one brigade of which had pierced the Federal line near an unfinished brick plantation house *(below)*.

Rallied by Major General John A. Logan and reinforced by a brigade from the XVI Corps, the Federals surged back and, in savage fighting, regained the lost ground.

"It was a trying moment to all who appreciated the situation," a Union soldier later recalled. "To fight to the bitter end was the only honorable alternative."

The panoramic view of that desperate combat is reproduced in its entirety here and on the following pages.

Illinois and Ohio troops of Colonel August Mersy's brigade mount a successful charge to retake captured Federal earthworks and the four guns of Captain Francis DeGress' Illinois battery. A soldier in Mersy's 81st Ohio wrote that "the boys started with wild yells that would have given credit to a tribe of Comanche Indians." The horses of DeGress' battery are caught in a fatal cross fire; their loss made it impossible for Manigault's Confederates to withdraw the captured guns.

Having guided the attacking Federal troops into position, Staff Lieutenant Edward Jonas *(above, on horseback)* glances back at his onrushing comrades. Colonel Mersy is barely visible behind a bush, his hat flying as he pitches headlong from his dying horse near the end of a footbridge *(foreground)*. One soldier recalled that the wounded Mersy "lamented not a little for his poor *Billy.*" In the middle distance, two brigades from Brigadier General Charles Woods's division of the XV Corps charge downhill to strike the Confederate left flank.

Waving his hat, General John (Black Jack) Logan (*above*) leads his staff to the scene of heaviest fighting. Logan had just taken command of the Federal Army of the Tennessee from the slain Major General James McPherson, and to one admiring soldier he seemed "a human hurricane on horseback." Immediately behind Logan, Captain Francis DeGress leaps his horse over a fallen infantryman. On the hillside above, a Federal ambulance bears wounded Brigadier General Manning Force to the rear.

Behind the Federal line, stragglers and wounded seek shelter along the damaged tracks of the Georgia Railroad. The yellow flag flying at middle distance identifies the cabin to both sides as a field hospital. On the horizon, near the granite dome of Stone Mountain, smoke rises from a cavalry engagement in progress at Decatur, six miles east of Atlanta.

Rallying grimly from an earlier repulse, the six Federal regiments of Brigadier General Joseph Lightburn's brigade move forward to regain their captured trenches. "It was impossible to preserve organizations intact," reported one of Lightburn's officers, "and regiments were completely intermixed and mingled." At right behind the attacking troops are the ambulances of the Federal XVII Corps.

Troops on the left flank of Lightburn's brigade charge through a wheat field (*foreground*), heading for the front line. In the middle distance, the 1st Iowa Battery gallops past a stone tannery to support Brigadier General William Harrow's beleaguered division (*right*). "Bring forward your caissons," Harrow ordered the battery's commander. "We will all go to hell together."

Mounted Federal officers (*foreground*) confer near a damaged wagon. The horse of Colonel Willard Warner rears at the sight of a dead man, and Colonel Wells Jones, commanding a brigade in the XV Corps, salutes Brigadier General Morgan Smith, who has just succeeded General Logan as corps commander. In the background, Major General Carter Stevenson's Confederates charge across open ground toward the wooded slope of Bald Hill.

Union Colonel James Martin, astride a gray horse, looks rearward for reinforcements as his brigade charges into wooded terrain near the captured Federal earthworks. Near the colonel, and behind the embattled lines of the 57th Ohio and the 111th Illinois, Federal soldiers hurry a clutch of Confederate prisoners to the rear. On their third try, the Federals succeeded in retaking the works.

Georgians of Colonel Abda Johnson's brigade charge downhill from their trenches to engage Martin's Federals in close combat. One Confederate officer has been carried into the enemy lines by his stampeding horse. Behind him, soldiers grapple for the flag of the 55th Illinois. "It was a desperate struggle, a struggle for life," one Federal recalled. "Men fought with bayonet and with breech, with a determination which knew no yielding."

Portraying History on a Grand Scale

The product of nearly a year's work, *The Battle of Atlanta* was created by the American Panorama Company of Milwaukee. The firm had been established in 1883 by William Wehner, an Austrian emigré who recognized the entertainment value of cycloramas and recruited more than a dozen German artists who had made a name for themselves painting grandiose scenes of the Franco-Prussian War.

In the summer of 1885, three of Wehner's artists traveled to Atlanta, where they sketched and photographed battlefield terrain from atop a 40-foot tower. Back in the Panorama Company's huge Milwaukee studio, the sketches were enlarged and trans-

"ATLANTA'S PET."

CYCLORAMA.

Working from a movable scaffold *(right)*, *Atlanta's* artists used a rapid assembly-line technique. Some painted the landscape, others the human figures and still others the horses. After a multicity tour, the finished painting opened in 1892 in Atlanta, where it was displayed in a circular building *(above)* that had housed earlier cycloramas.

Harper's Weekly who had been present at the battle, served as historical consultant. He ensured that the final painting was as accurate as it was spectacular.

Cycloramas were usually enhanced by blending three-dimensional figures and terrain into the foreground, although the sculpted parts at Atlanta (*above*) were not added until the 1930s. Civil War veterans sat as models for many of the painting's thousands of individual portraits (*left*). Other faces were adapted from wartime photographs.

Hood Fights Back

Now that John Bell Hood possessed what he had so avidly sought — at the age of 33, promotion to full general and command of the Army of Tennessee — he seemed strangely reluctant to seize control. The news from Richmond on that Sunday night, July 17, "so astounded and overwhelmed" him, he wrote later, that he "remained in deep thought throughout the night."

Before dawn on Monday, two members of Hood's staff helped their crippled commander to mount his horse and strapped him into the saddle. Then Hood rode to Joseph Johnston's headquarters northwest of Atlanta with an unusual request. He wanted Johnston to retain command until the military crisis had passed. "Pocket that dispatch," he pleaded with Johnston, "leave me in command of my corps and fight the battle for Atlanta."

But Johnston refused to postpone the change of command. So did President Jefferson Davis, despite a joint telegram from Hood and the other two corps commanders urging him to delay the order "until the fate of Atlanta is decided."

Johnston departed that afternoon, bound for Macon, where he and his wife, Lydia, took up temporary residence. Before he left, however, the troops poured out their admiration for the jaunty little general who had restored their hope the previous winter at Dalton and who had retained their loving respect even in retreat.

Several of his old regiments marched out the Marietta road that morning to take up new positions north of Atlanta near Peachtree Creek. When they reached the two-story white house that had served as Johnston's headquarters, the general stepped outside.

"He stood with head uncovered," wrote Colonel James C. Nisbet of the 66th Georgia. "We lifted our hats. There was no cheering! We simply passed silently, with heads uncovered. Some of the officers broke ranks and grasped his hand, as the tears poured down their cheeks."

Hood's regret at Johnston's quick departure stemmed less from personal affection than from his reluctance to deal with the perilous situation confronting his army. With the enemy threatening the city, two of his three top generals — Alexander Stewart, who now led Polk's former corps, and Benjamin F. Cheatham, whom Hood had named to lead his own corps temporarily — were untested in high command. And his one veteran corps commander, William Hardee, was so miffed at being passed over for command of the army that he asked for a transfer; his request was turned down.

Hood himself, though a superb commander at the division level, had yet to prove himself at managing large numbers of troops. "Hood is a bold fighter," his old chief, Robert E. Lee, had wired the President before the change. "I am doubtful as to other qualities necessary."

Hood's physical infirmities — his shat-

This sword and scabbard were carried into battle at Peachtree Creek on July 20, 1864, by Colonel George Cobham Jr., commander of the 111th Pennsylvania. His flank threatened, Cobham was brandishing the sword and calling on his men to change front when he was shot through the lungs. He died that evening.

tered left arm and missing right leg—cast doubt on his ability to lead an army. By the accounts of some contemporaries, Hood suffered such intense pain that he was taking laudanum, an opiate that could impair mental judgment.

Whatever the truth of this surmise, Hood had been known as headstrong and rash long before giving an arm and a leg for the Confederacy. As soon as William Sherman learned of the change in command—from a Southern newspaper smuggled out of Atlanta by a spy—he consulted two of his army commanders, James McPherson and John Schofield, who had known Hood intimately at West Point in the class of 1853.

Schofield had roomed with Hood and helped prevent his expulsion by tutoring him in mathematics. He warned Sherman that Hood would attack: "He'll hit you like hell, now, before you know it."

Though Sherman immediately cautioned his division commanders, he professed to be pleased. After 10 frustrating weeks of trying to trap the elusive Johnston, he welcomed the prospect of fighting "in open ground, on anything like equal terms, instead of being forced to run up against prepared entrenchments."

Sherman soon got his chance. On Tuesday, July 19—the day after Hood reluctantly took charge of the Confederate army—the new commander saw a flaw in the Federal alignment and made his first move.

The Federal armies, from their bridgeheads across the Chattahoochee, were now converging on Atlanta in a broad arc. Sherman intended to sever the Georgia Railroad, which ran from Atlanta eastward to Augusta and then made connections north to Richmond. By so doing, he could prevent the Confederates from receiving reinforcements from Lee's army in Virginia.

On Tuesday, McPherson's Army of the Tennessee was astride that railroad, marching toward Atlanta from Decatur, six miles to the east, destroying the rails as it came. Schofield's Army of the Ohio, connecting with McPherson's right, was heading toward Atlanta along a road a mile or so north of the railroad and parallel with it. And George Thomas' Army of the Cumberland was much farther to Schofield's right. Marching south, Thomas' troops were nearing Peachtree Creek, behind which the bulk of Hood's Confederates were deployed on ridges.

As Hood quickly perceived, the gap between the advancing armies of Thomas and Schofield was more than two miles wide. Moreover, a maze of small streams—headwaters of Peachtree Creek—laced the marshy ground in and around the gap, making necessary a roundabout detour if one Federal army had to come to the aid of the other. This situation gave Hood an opportunity that he now planned to exploit.

Hood outlined a plan at a meeting Tuesday night at his headquarters on Whitehall Street in Atlanta. He proposed to take advantage of the Federal gap by attacking on Wednesday with the corps of Hardee and Stewart when Thomas' army was crossing Peachtree Creek. These two corps were to drive Thomas' lead elements into the creek, oblique to the left, and crush the remainder of Thomas' troops in the pocket formed by the confluence of the creek and the Chattahoochee River.

Meanwhile, on the right of the Confederate line, Cheatham's corps — with the help of the cavalry and the state militia — would hold off McPherson and Schofield. Then, after Thomas was defeated, Hardee and Stewart would join Cheatham in destroying the other two Federal armies.

The prospect of defeating Sherman greatly excited Hood. A reporter who talked with him after the meeting wrote that the general's eyes flashed with "a strange indescribable light."

But the upcoming battle would be Hood's first as an independent commander, and he made some mistakes in coordinating the attack. First, although he hoped to catch Thomas' columns while they were crossing the creek and before they could entrench, he unaccountably scheduled Wednesday's attack for the comparatively late hour of 1 p.m. Then, on Wednesday, readjustments in the Confederate corps alignment caused a further delay of two hours.

It was almost 4 p.m. by the time Hood's assault formations finally started forward from their fortifications a mile south of Peachtree Creek. By then, most of Thomas' Federals had crossed to the south bank, and the opportunity to catch the Army of the Cumberland athwart the creek had been lost.

Confederate mistakes persisted. Hood's plan called for the assault to be made in eche-

lon by three of Hardee's divisions and two of Stewart's, with each corps retaining a division in reserve. Hardee's rightmost division under William Bate would attack first. When it had advanced about 150 yards, the next division on the left would follow — and so on in stairstep succession.

This textbook maneuver fell apart quickly. Some of Stewart's men jumped the gun, preceding Hardee's main attack, and then the divisions advanced pell-mell with little regard for the precise timing Hood had envisioned.

And yet, despite all the delays and the Confederates' lack of coordination, the attack caught the Federals off guard.

Thomas had seven divisions on an irregular front about three miles wide and roughly parallel to Peachtree Creek. It was a hot, lazy day, and only General John Newton, commanding the easternmost division, had been concerned enough to halt and throw up temporary breastworks.

The rest of the Federal troops either were still moving up or had just stopped and were sprawled about resting, playing cards or picking blackberries. The men of the 123rd New York had gotten word they would probably camp for the night where they were. "We were congratulating ourselves on this unexpected good luck," wrote Sergeant Rice Bull, "when suddenly there was a rifle shot on our front. It was as unexpected as would be thunder from out of a clear sky."

Hardee's attack slammed into the four divisions on Thomas' left. Newton's men, deployed on a ridge astride the Peachtree road about a half mile south of the creek, got a double dose. His troops were hit in front by William Walker's division and in the left

General John Bell Hood was lionized in the South for the headlong charges he led at Gaines's Mill, Gettysburg and Chickamauga — the last of which cost him his right leg. Yet some prewar Army men thought him too careless for high command: In his senior year at West Point, he had garnered 196 demerits, only four short of the number requiring dismissal.

ments of defensive crisis. Now he swung into action. He called up a battery and hurried the horses across the bridge, slapping them with his hand as they passed. The battery was joined in line by six of Newton's guns and four of his regiments, which had redeployed to face east in front of the bridge.

The Federals opened fire as Bate's men emerged from the thickets and started to rush across open ground to the bridge. The concentration of fire broke the charging Confederate columns. "The leading companies, or what was left of them, surged backward upon those in the rear," wrote a soldier of the 125th Ohio. "They in turn broke, and then all went in wild disorder back to the friendly cover of the timber."

Newton, having repulsed the assaults on his left flank and front, faced a new threat on his right. The adjoining division under Brigadier General William T. Ward, posted behind a ridge several hundred yards in the rear, had not come in line; Ward's absence had created a quarter-mile-wide gap between Newton's right and the next Union division. Into this pocket marched Cheatham's division under the temporary command of Brigadier General George E. Maney.

As Newton's men hurriedly faced right to enfilade this Confederate wedge, a crucial conversation was occurring behind the Federal line. Two of General Ward's brigade commanders — Colonel John Coburn and Colonel Benjamin Henry Harrison, the future President — appealed to Ward for permission to move their men forward. Ward at first refused, saying that it was against the orders of his corps commander, General Joseph Hooker; but at the last possible moment Ward relented and permitted the counterattack to proceed.

flank by Bate's. Federal teamsters climbed trees in the rear and reported that "the Johnnies" were "charging by the acre."

Bate's troops poured around Newton's left. Struggling through thickets and swampy ground, the columns routed two Federal regiments, which escaped only by plunging into Peachtree Creek and swimming to the north bank.

The Federal commander, George Thomas, watched from the north bank of the creek with growing apprehension. The attackers were headed directly toward a crucial bridge over the creek in Newton's left rear; if they captured it, the main Federal line of withdrawal would be severed. Never known for alacrity — "Old Slow Trot," some called him for his refusal ever to hurry his horse — Thomas was always at his best in such mo-

Battle of Peach-tree Creek July 20th, 64
General Jo. Hooker's 20th corps

Atlanta Campaign

attack of Hardee + Stewart's corps
on the army of the Cumberland.
4 miles north of Atlanta.

Harrison sent his men forward; supported by Coburn's troops, he "put spurs to his horse and dashed forward up the hill, in front of his brigade," wrote a witness. "Both brigades cheering ran rapidly up the hill."

Ward's remaining brigade followed, and the sudden appearance of the entire division on the crest of the ridge threw the Confederate assault into confusion. "Meeting my line of battle seemed to completely addle their brains," reported Ward.

Little by little, the Confederates were forced to yield ground until a final lunge gained the Federals control of the ridge and the surrounding fields.

Back on the north bank of the creek, George Thomas awaited the outcome of this fight, worriedly working his short, thick whiskers "all out of shape," according to one observer. But when he saw Maney's Confederates break in front of Ward's men, he threw his hat to the ground in delight and shouted, "Hurrah! Look at the Third Division. They're driving them!"

The Harrison-led charge mended the breach on the Federal front; farther west down Thomas' line, in savage fighting, the Confederates were able to penetrate the defenses in places but they could make no lasting gains. After two hours of fighting, the Confederate attack was stymied — from Hardee's own corps on the right to Stewart's corps on the left. It was time for William Hardee to play his trump card. All afternoon

In this tattered sketch penned by artist Theodore Davis near Peachtree Creek on July 20, Major General Joseph Hooker (*mounted, in foreground*) heeds an aide peering through a field glass as troops of Hooker's XX Corps form alongside their battle flags to meet the approaching Confederates. "When that horrible mass of Johnnies struck our line," one of Hooker's men recalled, "we found them six deep."

he had kept in reserve the toughest division in Hood's army—that of Patrick Cleburne. Now Hardee decided to unleash Cleburne against Thomas' far left with the hope that he could salvage a victory.

At 6 p.m., just as Cleburne got his men in line for the assault, a courier came galloping up with urgent orders from Hood. McPherson's Army of the Tennessee was advancing on Atlanta with alarming speed. At noon these Federals had been midway between Decatur and Atlanta, well within artillery range of the city, and McPherson had ordered the first artillery bombardment. Captain Francis DeGress of Battery H, 1st Illinois Light Artillery, unlimbered one of his 20-pounder Parrotts and fired the first shot.

The shell arched over the woods and fell about two and a half miles away at the intersection of Ivy and Ellis Streets. A little girl walking there with her parents and her dog was killed instantly—Atlanta's first civilian casualty of the campaign. Now McPherson's troops were threatening to flank Joseph Wheeler's cavalry off a patch of high ground near the Georgia Railroad a few miles east of Atlanta. Hood needed a division of infantry to support Wheeler. So Hardee reluctantly called off Cleburne and sent him marching southeastward to block McPherson.

Cleburne's departure and the approach of darkness ended the Battle of Peachtree Creek. Hood's first gamble in his new command had failed. He had gained not an inch of ground, and his troops had suffered nearly 3,000 casualties—a large price when compared with the Federal toll of about 1,700.

The ridge where Cleburne reinforced Wheeler's cavalry on Wednesday night was bare of trees and was thereby called Bald Hill. And because it commanded the eastern approach to Atlanta, Bald Hill became the focus of the following day's fighting—and then the key to the battle.

At daybreak on Thursday, July 21, McPherson's artillery opened up against Cleburne and Wheeler on and around the hill. The Confederates were particularly hard-hit by the 20-pounder Parrotts of Captain DeGress, who had fired the first shells into Atlanta the previous day.

"I have never before witnessed such accurate and destructive cannonading," reported Brigadier General James A. Smith, who led Cleburne's Texas Brigade. "In a few minutes 40 men were killed and over 100 wounded by this battery alone. In the Eighteenth Texas Cavalry, dismounted, 17 of the 18 men composing one company were placed hors de combat by one shot alone."

After the bombardment, Federal infantry moved forward. A brigade of Brigadier General Mortimer Leggett's division, under Brigadier General Manning Force, stormed the hill, supported on the right by a division under Brigadier General Giles Smith.

Thursday was so hot that three Federal officers fell from sunstroke on the slopes of the hill; the action was so furious that Patrick Cleburne called it "the bitterest fighting" of his life. By afternoon, the Federals had control of the crest—at a cost of 750 casualties—and had begun emplacing artillery there. From this strong point, McPherson's guns could command the Confederate extreme right flank.

To John Bell Hood, it was clear that McPherson was now in a position to flank the Confederate right on the south and march into Atlanta practically unimpeded. Or McPherson could skirt the southern edge of the city and strike westward for the Macon &

LIEUTENANT GEORGE YOUNG

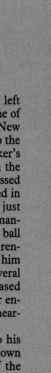

List of Articles lost & destroyed in the Public Service near Atlanta Ga. while in the possession of Lt. Ge Young in the Month of July 1864

No	Articles	Circumstances & cause
1	Horse	The horse was Killed in the
1	Halter & Strap	Battle of Peach Tree creek July 20th 1864 and the halter was on the horse & I was wounded & prevented from saving the same

I certify that the several Articles above mentioned have been unavoidably lost or destroyed while in the public Service as indicated by the remarks annexed to them respectively

Lt. Ge Young
Pro. Mar. 3rd Brig.

STATEMENT OF LOSSES

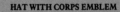

HAT WITH CORPS EMBLEM

The Sad Legacy of a Courier's Last Run

The savage struggle at Peachtree Creek left its mark on many of the participants, one of them a young lieutenant with the 143rd New York named George Young. Attached to the staff of Colonel James Robinson in Hooker's corps, Young was riding as a courier in the heat of the battle when a Minié ball passed through the body of his horse and lodged in Young's right leg, splintering two bones just below the knee. His regimental surgeon managed to salvage the limb, removing the ball and dressing the wound, but the injury rendered Young unfit for duty and plagued him for the rest of his days. He underwent several operations in later life to remove diseased bone tissue; finally in March 1909, after enduring the pain of chronic infection for nearly 45 years, Young died of his wound.

Among the effects he bequeathed to his descendants was the Federal uniform shown here, including a haunting emblem of the price Young paid for the Union: a pair of blue trousers, torn by the ball that ended his service.

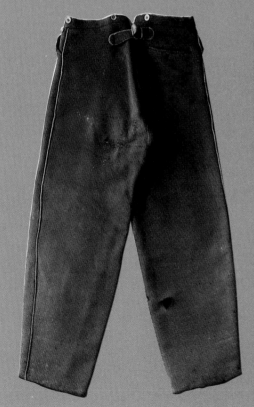

BULLET-RENT TROUSERS

LIEUTENANT'S FROCK COAT

Western Railroad, Atlanta's most important remaining supply line, and thus isolate both the city and Hood's army.

To forestall these possibilities, Hood presented a daring plan to his commanders Thursday night. In conception, it borrowed from those brilliant flanking marches in Virginia—designed by Robert E. Lee and executed by Stonewall Jackson—that got in the rear of the Federal armies at Second Bull Run and Chancellorsville.

Hood intended to get in the rear of McPherson's Army of the Tennessee. Although McPherson was solidly anchored on Bald Hill, his extreme left, farther south, was exposed. Unprotected by terrain or by a screen of cavalry to warn of impending attack, this flank was "up in the air," as military vernacular had it.

To cover his strike, Hood ordered two of his corps—Stewart's and Cheatham's—to withdraw that night into new fortifications bordering Atlanta on the north and east. Meanwhile, Hardee was to march his four divisions south through Atlanta and then turn northeastward to reach McPherson's rear. Wheeler's cavalry would accompany Hardee's infantry but then proceed to Decatur to destroy McPherson's wagon train, which was encamped in the woods just south of the little town.

At dawn on Friday, Hardee would hit McPherson's exposed left from flank and rear. When Hardee's attack was well under way, Cheatham would assault McPherson from the west. Once the young Federal general was caught and crunched in this vise, the Confederates would deal with the two remaining enemy armies.

Hood's plan required that Hardee make a difficult night march of more than 15 miles.

The march immediately fell behind schedule. Cleburne's troops had difficulty disengaging from the Federals at Bald Hill, and it was past midnight when his men finally broke contact and joined the rear of the column marching south through Atlanta.

There were further delays. Hardee's men were exhausted from the fighting and the oppressive heat. Stumbling along back roads in pitch darkness, they struggled to keep their feet; many fell by the wayside.

By dawn, only the vanguard of the weary column had reached the assembly point, a place three or four miles southwest of Decatur known as Widow Parker's farm. There, as the men came up during the morning, Hardee aligned his assault columns: four divisions abreast.

It was nearly noon when Hardee finally launched his approach march. Now the men had to negotiate formidable terrain before hitting the Federals—a morass two miles long with a big millpond and undergrowth so thick, Hardee wrote later, that he "could not see ten paces."

But as Hardee's divisions struggled to pass through the brier patches, losing their alignment, they at least seemed to be heading for the right place. When Hood in Atlanta got a dispatch from Hardee stating his readiness to attack, Hood jabbed his finger at a map and exclaimed: "Hardee is just where I wanted him!" Hardee had curved around McPherson's left flank and was moving north and northwest—into the Federal rear.

Hardee was where Sherman least expected to find him. Sherman did not anticipate another Confederate assault so soon after Peachtree Creek; and early Friday morning, when Federal pickets reported the Confeder-

Color Sergeant Fergus Elliott of the
109th Pennsylvania, wearing a XX
Corps badge here, saw duty as an artillerist at Peachtree Creek. With
Geary during a Confederate attack,
he spotted two abandoned Union
guns, rallied volunteers and directed
fire until the attackers retreated.

ates had abandoned their outer arc of fortifications north and east of the city, Sherman
actually thought Hood was evacuating Atlanta. In fact, this story reached several
Northern newspapers, which prematurely
proclaimed the fall of Atlanta.

Even after dawn, when the Federals
pressed forward to discover that the Confederates merely had taken up a new line nearer
the city, Sherman failed to show concern for
his exposed left. What obsessed him was
tearing up the Georgia Railroad east of the
city. The previous day Sherman had pulled
Kenner Garrard's cavalry division from Mc-
Pherson's flank and sent it 40 miles to the
east to rip up rails and destroy railroad
bridges at Covington.

While Sherman fretted about the railroad,
McPherson worried about what his old class-
mate Hood might do to his flank. About
7:30 Friday morning—while Hardee was
forming up undetected to the south—Mc-
Pherson ordered Grenville Dodge's XVI
Corps, which was waiting in reserve, to ex-
tend and strengthen the left, connecting with
Major General Francis Preston Blair's XVII
Corps below Bald Hill.

Shortly after Dodge started his march,
McPherson received a note from Sherman
negating the order. Sherman wanted Dodge,
who was a professional railroad engineer before the War, to put his entire corps to work
"destroying, absolutely, the railroad back to
and including Decatur."

But McPherson persevered. At midmorning, he rode north of the railroad to Sherman's headquarters. With his easy charm—
a West Point friend later wrote of McPherson's "sunny temper and warm heart"—he
managed to persuade his superior to permit
Dodge to go into line as originally ordered.

McPherson then inspected his two-mile front. Finding everything quiet, he had lunch with several generals in a little grove of oaks near the railroad. The generals were enjoying their cigars when, at 12:15 p.m., they heard the rattle of musketry a mile and a half to the southeast.

It was the sound of Federal pickets exchanging fire with Hardee's Confederates. Grenville Dodge heard the shots as well. Thanks to McPherson's perseverance with Sherman, Dodge happened to be in the right place to respond to them. He had two divisions behind McPherson's main line; one of them, under Thomas Sweeny, was halted near Sugar Creek, about a mile east of Bald Hill, awaiting orders to take position on the left flank farther south of the hill. The other division, Brigadier General John Fuller's, was nearby, just west of Sweeny.

When the firing broke out, Dodge was sitting down to lunch at Fuller's headquarters. He immediately ordered Fuller to get his division in line facing southeast, then galloped east to align Sweeny's men. He personally ordered regiments into place "as if he were a brigade commander or a mere colonel, cutting red tape all to pieces," observed Captain James Compton of the 52nd Illinois. Dodge deployed Sweeny's division with one brigade on the right facing southeast, two batteries on a ridge in the middle, and another brigade on the left facing east.

Dodge had fewer than 5,000 soldiers to stretch in a single line. His corps was actually only half a corps to begin with, and one of Fuller's two brigades was guarding the wagon trains at Decatur. But for once the defenders had the advantage of surprise. The two Confederate divisions emerging from the woods 300 yards from Dodge's line ex-pected to find the vulnerable Federal rear, not a line of battle on the alert. One of McPherson's staff officers, Lieutenant Colonel William Strong, watched the advance: "The scene at this time was grand impressive. It seemed to us that every mounted officer of the attacking column was riding at the front of, or on the right or left of, the first line of battle. The regimental colors waved and fluttered in advance of the lines and not a shot was fired by the rebel infantry."

Bate's division was on the Confederate right, and Walker's was on the left — but without Walker. That general, whom Joseph Johnston once pronounced the only officer fit to lead a division in the Western command, lay dead at the age of 47. Walker had fallen a few hundred yards back in the woods, the victim of a Federal picket who fired one of the first shots.

With Brigadier General Hugh Mercer now commanding Walker's division, the Confederates "came tearing wildly through the woods with the yells of demons," a Federal officer wrote. In three columns, the two divisions advanced into the open, halted and began to fire. "It was a square face-to-face grapple in open field, neither line advancing or retreating," wrote Colonel Robert N. Adams of the 81st Ohio.

The Confederates were supported by artillery posted behind them in the woods. But the Union guns — the 14th Ohio Battery and Battery H of the 1st Missouri — situated on the high ground in the middle of Sweeny's line had the better position. These 12 guns began pouring out the first of the more than 1,000 rounds of shell, case and canister they would fire that afternoon.

Wavering under this barrage, the Confederates retreated to the woods and re-formed.

Soon they came again. One of the attackers, Sergeant John Green of the 6th Kentucky, recalled, "They pour their lead into us; their batteries open on us slaying our men right and left." Dodge mounted counterattacks. One of Sweeny's regiments, the 81st Ohio, charged and captured 226 prisoners from Bate's division. Charges by two of Fuller's Ohio regiments on Dodge's right decimated the 66th Georgia of Walker's division — "All who were not shot, or did not run away, were captured," reported Fuller.

Although these counterattacks, together with devastating artillery fire, repulsed the second Confederate assault, Fuller then had trouble on his right flank. A gap of about 600 yards separated his single brigade from the left flank of McPherson's main line. A column of Confederates slipped into this wide space and opened an enfilading fire on Fuller's troops.

Fuller tried to change front to meet this threat. The maneuver involved an about-face, meaning that the Federals temporarily had their backs to the enemy. Worse, keeping their alignment on the broken ground was almost impossible. "For a moment," Fuller reported, "it appeared these veteran regiments would be routed."

Fearing that his men might stampede to the rear instead of halting at the proper time, Fuller seized the colors of his old regiment, the 27th Ohio. He planted the flag where he wanted to form the line and pointed with his sword to indicate the position to be taken.

The men of the 27th, shouting their approval, instantly formed on either side of the flag. Then, with the 39th Ohio on their left, they charged and drove the Confederates back toward the woods.

A few minutes later, Fuller saw a Confederate general ride forward, swinging his hat in an attempt to rally the men. "The next moment," Fuller reported, "his horse went back riderless." Fuller thought the fallen general was William Walker, but Walker had died an hour and a half earlier. The victim apparently was a brigadier general in Walker's division, States Rights Gist, who was reported wounded that afternoon.

From a hill north of the fighting, the commander of the Army of the Tennessee, James McPherson, had watched for more than an hour while Dodge's troops repulsed the Confederate assaults. Though one of his generals would later remark, "The Lord put Dodge in the right place today," that fortuitous piece of work was McPherson's, of course, and the young general must have felt a surge of pride.

Satisfied that Dodge could hold his own, McPherson turned his attention to the west, to the vulnerable left flank of General Blair's XVII Corps. He already had received several messages from Blair indicating that the division there, led by Brigadier General Giles A. Smith, was under attack.

Shortly before 2 p.m., McPherson decided to ride over to see for himself. In the company of several officers, he took a narrow road that led westward through the wooded gap separating Dodge's troops from Blair's. Spotting a defensible ridge on the left of the road, McPherson ordered his aide, Lieutenant Colonel William Strong, to ride north to XV Corps near the railroad and bring one of John Logan's reserve brigades to this ridge to plug the gap.

McPherson looked "straight as an arrow," Strong recalled later, "a smile lighting his handsome face, and his eye full of the fire of

Shortly after noon on July 22, Hardee's Confederate corps attacked McPherson's army south of the Georgia Railroad. The two divisions on Hardee's right, under Bate and Walker, nearly flanked McPherson's main line but met unexpected resistance from Dodge's XVI Corps. To Walker's left, meanwhile, Cleburne's division found a gap in the Federal line and pushed north to Bald Hill, threatening the Federals from the rear before being checked in desperate fighting.

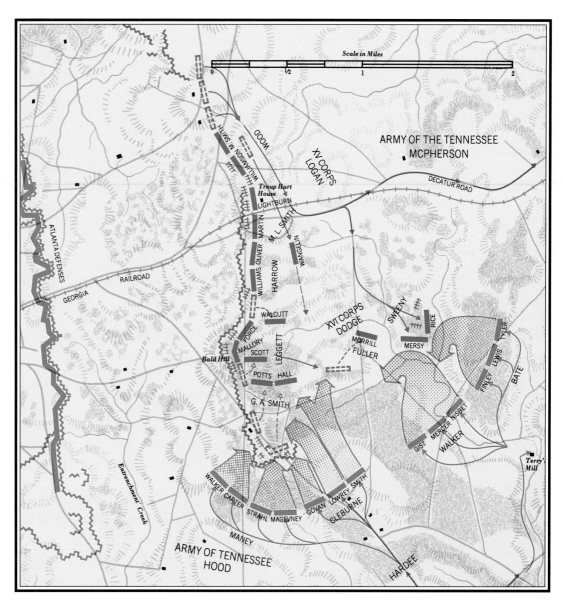

battle." McPherson called out to Strong as they parted, "Join me at Giles Smith's." Then the army commander galloped southwest down the road on the black horse that had carried him through dozens of actions since the Battle of Shiloh.

McPherson went only 150 yards before he met a company of Confederates — skirmishers from Patrick Cleburne's division.

The grayclad commander, Captain Richard Beard of the 5th Confederate Regiment, raised his sword as a signal for McPherson to surrender. But McPherson was not to be taken so easily. "He checked his horse slightly," wrote Beard, "raised his hat as politely as if he was saluting a lady, wheeled his horse's head directly to the right and dashed off to the rear in a full gallop."

Beard ordered his men to open fire. McPherson was riding under a low-hanging tree limb, bending over his horse's neck. A bullet hit him in the lower back and ranged upward, passing near his heart. McPherson fell to the ground, mortally wounded.

The same volley unhorsed a Federal signal officer, William H. Sherfy, who was trailing McPherson, dashing him unconscious against a tree. His watch, which was crushed by the impact, stopped at 2:02 p.m.

Beard knew at once from McPherson's blood-soaked uniform that he had bagged a high-ranking Federal.

"Who is this man lying here?" he inquired of Colonel Robert K. Scott, a XVII Corps brigade commander who, like the signal officer, had been trailing McPherson and was unhorsed by the same Confederate volley.

Scott looked up at Beard with tears in his eyes. "Sir, it is General McPherson," he responded. "You have killed the best man in our army."

Beard sent to the rear the captives of McPherson's contingent. Then, thinking McPherson dead, Beard left the general lying there and moved forward into battle, where he soon became a captive himself.

McPherson in fact was still alive. He survived long enough — 20 minutes or so — for a wounded Federal prisoner, Private George Reynolds of the 15th Iowa, to discover him and comfort his final moments by cradling a blanket under his head and moistening his lips with water.

Soon thereafter, one of Fuller's regiments, the 64th Illinois, faced right and charged into the wooded gap. The Illinois men captured 40 Confederates and found in one captive's haversack McPherson's wallet, which contained a dispatch from Sherman detailing plans for the next day's operations. The Illinois men held the ground long enough to permit the recovery of McPherson's body, which was then borne by ambulance to Sherman's headquarters.

There the body was laid out on a door someone had wrenched from its hinges to serve as a bier. Sherman wept unashamedly over his fallen protégé — only 35 years old — whom he had thought one day would succeed him and Grant in the Union high command. Suddenly, random Confederate shells started hitting the headquarters, and Sherman realized the old wooden house might catch fire. He covered the body with a United States flag and ordered the slain general sent to safety at Marietta.

Despite his obvious grief, Sherman maintained the remarkable calm that came over him in a crisis. "He had the rare faculty of being more equable under great responsibilities and scenes of great excitement," wrote Major General Jacob D. Cox. "At such times his eccentricities disappeared. His mind seemed never so clear, his confidence never so strong, his spirit never so inspiring, and his temper never so amiable as in the crisis of some fierce struggle like that of the day when McPherson fell in front of Atlanta."

Sherman managed to stay in close touch with a separate engagement at Decatur. Joseph Wheeler's Confederate cavalrymen, fighting dismounted and with fierce valor, had driven a brigade of Fuller's division under John W. Sprague from town. But Sherman sent a brigade of reinforcements from Schofield's army that arrived in time to protect the army's wagon trains.

Meanwhile, Sherman already had provided for the succession of McPherson. At first word that McPherson's horse had

Below, in a painting by James Taylor, reproduced in black and white, General Grenville Dodge gestures to an officer to the right of the XVI Corps flag at a critical moment in the battle for Atlanta. By deploying Thomas Sweeny's force himself, Dodge drew the ire of Sweeny, the one-armed general standing at left, with his sleeve pinned to his jacket, beside a fallen horse. But Dodge was less concerned with protocol than with the threat to Fuller's brigade *(below, right background)*, shown on a larger scale by Taylor in another scene *(inset, right)*. Here, Fuller plants the flag to mark a new line for his men.

emerged from the woods riderless, he ordered John Logan of XV Corps to take command of the Army of the Tennessee. And when Logan sent word that his new command was hard pressed, Sherman replied: "Tell General Logan to fight 'em, fight 'em, fight 'em like hell!"

At midafternoon, Logan was being pressured on the extreme left flank, where Giles Smith's division was under assault by Patrick Cleburne's troops.

Cleburne had launched his attack about 30 minutes after Bate and Walker hit Dodge's XVI Corps nearly a half mile to the east. George Maney's division was supposed to support Cleburne, but Maney's columns ran afoul of the rough terrain and their attack was late and uncoordinated. Cleburne's troops swept north, expecting to come upon an unprotected Federal flank. Much to their surprise, they hit the southern tip of Smith's line where it curved back to the east in the shape of a hook. Federal entrenchments and a nearly impassable abatis of slashed young oak trees extended across the road in front of Cleburne's men.

Cleburne's leftmost brigade, Arkansas men under Brigadier General Daniel C. Govan, greatly overlapped Smith's uncovered left flank. While half of Govan's brigade pushed head on through the abatis, the other half swung around to the right in an attempt to pass and turn Smith's flank.

The Confederates executing the flanking movement found the wooded gap between Smith and Dodge. About 2 p.m. they reached the road where, at that very moment, James McPherson was galloping to his death farther east. On that road, they intercepted and seized six guns of Battery F, 2nd U.S. Artillery, which was hurrying east to aid Dodge's XVI Corps.

Then Govan's Arkansans turned back to the west and cut off part of the Federal force — the Iowa brigade of Giles Smith's division — that was fronting south. The Confederates captured two additional Federal guns and 700 Iowans of Colonel William W. Belknap's brigade, including an entire regiment, the 16th Iowa. In the process they liberated 75 Arkansans, who had surrendered to the Iowans only minutes before.

Reunited, Govan's brigade pushed north, driving Smith's shattered flank back toward Bald Hill. As the Federal line was compressed, many of Smith's men were compelled to change front repeatedly. From behind their breastworks, which faced west toward Atlanta, they had to front south against Govan and then east to cope with an additional threat.

This danger was posed by Cleburne's Texas Brigade under Brigadier General James A. Smith. The Texans, attacking north on Govan's right, poured into the wooded gap and

A Baptist minister's son whose only prewar tactical training was drilling militia, Brigadier General John Fuller showed great composure under fire at Atlanta. Pressed on front and flank, he braced his men with what one of them termed his "calm, musical, reassuring voice," repeating the injunction: "Steady, boys, steady."

wreaked havoc — some of them were responsible for McPherson's death. While part of the Texas Brigade turned left and attacked Giles Smith's division from the rear, another element moved right and engaged the flank of Fuller's division.

Hurrying northward between 2 and 3 p.m. with what James Smith called "ungovernable enthusiasm," the Texans got all the way behind Bald Hill. Thus, in little more than 24 hours, these men had come virtually full circle. The previous day they had defended Bald Hill against the Federal division of Mortimer Leggett. Now, from Leggett's former positions, the Texans were attempting to retake the height.

Leggett's Federals, menaced from the rear, had to leap their breastworks and face east to meet the Texans. In this confusing state of affairs, compounded by smoke obscuring the field, Leggett's men worried that their comrades flanking the hill might mistake them for Confederates and open fire.

To dispel any doubt about who controlled the hill, the brigade commander, Manning F. Force, called for a flag to mark his line. One of his young officers, assuming that the situation was so hopeless the general meant to surrender, went looking for a white handkerchief or shirt. "Damn you, sir!" Force shouted. "I don't want a flag of *truce;* I want the American flag!"

A few minutes later, a bullet passed through Force's head, narrowly missing his brain but shattering his palate and leaving him unable to speak. Force's men carried on and, with the support of 10 artillery pieces posted on and near the hill, repeatedly beat back the Texans' charges.

Cleburne's Texans soon faced danger from another direction. A punishing enfilade of musketry on their right flank erupted from Brigadier General Charles C. Walcutt's brigade of the Federal XV Corps, which had turned south to aid Leggett.

By about 3 p.m., the Texans' commander, James Smith, was wounded, and all but one of their regimental commanders was out of action. The Texans had suffered enough. Disheartened and virtually leaderless, they relaxed the pressure against Bald Hill. Half of one regiment, the 5th Confederate, surrendered. Others fell back southward to take up positions in support of Govan's brigade.

From his observation post on the second floor of a house a mile or so west of Bald Hill, John Bell Hood viewed the Battle of Atlanta with growing anger. Looking to the southeast, he had watched with what he later termed "astonishment and bitter disappointment." Hood was first upset because the assault, scheduled to start at dawn, got under way six hours late. Then — mistakenly — he assumed that Hardee had failed to get in the rear of the Federal line (Hood evidently could not see the attacks east of McPherson's main line).

In fact, Hood himself was guilty of the day's most serious failure in command. Though he had watched Cleburne push the Federals north toward Bald Hill, he unaccountably delayed for nearly two hours the second phase of his battle plan: an assault from the west by Cheatham's three divisions.

Finally, about 3 p.m., Hood decided to create what he later called "a diversion" to aid Hardee. He ordered Cheatham to attack.

By the time Cheatham advanced, it was 3:30 p.m. and the high tide of Hardee's assaults had ebbed. On both of Hardee's fronts — south and east of Bald Hill and farther east at Sugar Creek — his Confederates were falling back and regrouping after nearly three hours of hard fighting. Unaware of this, Cheatham's fresh troops advanced with undiminished vigor on a front more than a mile wide, extending from Bald Hill on the south to a point about 500 yards north of the Georgia Railroad.

On their right, at Bald Hill, they found the going rough. Leggett's Federals, having scarcely caught their breath after repulsing Cleburne to their rear, jumped back across their breastworks to face west — "looking for all the world," wrote a Federal officer, "like a long line of those toy-monkeys you see which jump over the end of a stick."

The Federals held off Cheatham with such grit that they proudly began referring to this treeless high ground as Leggett's Hill, in honor of their division commander.

It was another story a half mile north of the hill, where Cheatham attacked on both sides of the railroad with two divisions supported by long-range artillery. The terrain here was relatively flat, and the defenders — the three divisions of Logan's old XV Corps — had been considerably weakened by the earlier dispatch of troops to bolster Dodge's XVI Corps at Sugar Creek.

The most vulnerable part of the Federal line was held by the division of Brigadier General Morgan L. Smith, Giles Smith's older brother, who had temporarily replaced Logan as corps commander. Now manned by only a half-dozen regiments, Smith's thin line straddled the railroad cut — an excavation 15 feet deep and 50 feet wide at the top.

Cheatham's advance against Smith's line was spearheaded by Brigadier General John C. Brown's division — the brigade of Arthur M. Manigault on the left of the railroad and that of Colonel John G. Coltart on the right. Manigault's men quickly captured a two-gun section of Battery A, 1st Illinois Artillery, posted in the skirmish line well in advance of the Federal main line. But then the Confederate line began shifting "like the movements of a serpent," Manigault wrote, and his brigade suffered a repulse; the men took cover in a ravine. Beyond the ravine, on a wagon road that ran just north of the railroad and parallel with it, stood the large white wooden house of the Widow Pope.

Men from Manigault's 10th South Carolina, together with soldiers from the 19th South Carolina, got into the house. They climbed to the second floor and, from windows and veranda, poured down a commanding fire on the Federal main line 200 yards in front of them. Their sharpshooting was particularly galling to the crews of six Federal guns flanking both sides of the railroad cut. These guns returned the fire, blanketing the field with dense clouds of smoke.

The smoke concealed Manigault's columns, which massed near the Pope house

Pictured here as a captain early in the War, Confederate Colonel James Nisbet was taken prisoner by Fuller's troops on the 22nd as he led the 66th Georgia forward. When a young Ohioan guarding him said that Nisbet did not seem frightened at the prospect of captivity, he responded: "I have captured thousands of your men since the war commenced, and always treated them right." The Ohioan pledged to do likewise.

Major General James McPherson takes a shot in the back as he attempts to elude capture by Confederate skirmishers on the afternoon of the 22nd. McPherson became the only commander of a Federal army to die in battle during the War.

and then rushed forward on the road and in the cover afforded by the railroad cut. Before the Federals realized what had happened, these Confederate columns suddenly emerged 75 yards in the rear of the Federal works. The air was filled with "bullets madly hissing from the front, bullets spitefully whizzing from the rear," noted Lieutenant George Bailey of the 6th Missouri, who soon fell into Confederate hands. Colonel Coltart's men had drifted to the right, where they came under heavy flanking fire from the Federal main line; nevertheless, they were able to seize a portion of the enemy entrenchments.

Behind the cut, the Federal line was thrown into hopeless confusion. Manigault's Confederates took four guns to the left of the railroad cut. The Mississippi brigade of Colonel Jacob H. Sharp, following in Manigault's wake, pushed into the cut, turned right and captured the two remaining Federal guns. Then they drove the Federal troops a half mile from their lines. Lieutenant R. M. Gill of the 41st Mississippi wrote: "We charged with an awful yell but few Yankees staid to see the racket. I never saw the like of knapsacks, blankets, oil cloths and canteens in my life."

Manigault's troops, meanwhile, advanced about 200 yards north of the cut to drive away the infantry supporting Francis De-Gress' celebrated Illinois battery.

DeGress, alone with his crews, desperately turned the guns to the left and greeted the enemy charge with double canister. When the Confederates kept coming, he ordered his men to safety but stayed on with Sergeant

107

Peter Wyman to begin spiking the guns.

Their job was half-finished when the Confederates pushed to within 20 paces. DeGress was standing defiantly between his last two working guns with a lanyard in each hand. He answered the Confederate order to surrender by firing both pieces at point-blank range.

Then, obscured by the smoke, he and Wyman spiked those two guns and made a dash for the rear. Wyman died in a volley of bullets; DeGress somehow escaped unhurt to

report to Sherman — in tears — the loss of his beloved guns.

The retreating Federal infantry regrouped 400 yards to the rear, taking up position in a line they had occupied the day before. But their withdrawal opened a gap that exposed the flanks of the Federal divisions on either side, and Cheatham's troops poured in to widen the wedge.

To the south, the blueclads occupying the right of William Harrow's division yielded ground — but grudgingly. In the fierce fight-

Seated at right, above, with members of his staff, Brigadier General Manning Force was awarded the Medal of Honor for his actions at Bald Hill — a position he took by storm on the 21st and fell wounded defending the next day. An enlisted man who drilled under Force recalled him as a "spare, grave man with an eye that penetrated to the spine of a culprit." The soldier continued: "Force took the deepest interest in our welfare and so was very strict with our follies."

Around 3 p.m. on the 22nd, with Hardee's Confederates stalled to the south, Hood at last committed the bulk of Cheatham's corps to the offensive. While Carter Stevenson's division pressed the Federals on Bald Hill from the west, Arthur Manigault's brigade broke through the XV Corps line along the railroad. But the Union's General Logan — succeeding the fallen McPherson — proved equal to the occasion, shoring up his right and beating back this final thrust.

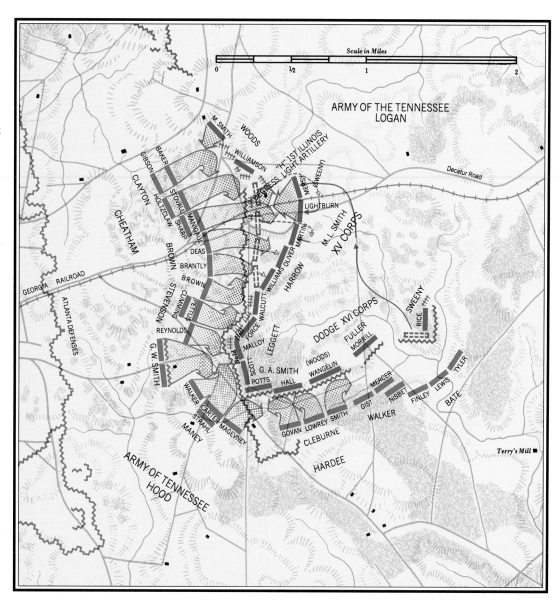

ing, a Confederate officer demanded the surrender of a soldier from the 97th Indiana; the Federal turned and shot the officer, then drove his bayonet into another would-be captor. The wounded Confederate grabbed a spade and began beating the defiant Federal. A third Confederate entered the fray and ended it, though not the Hoosier's life, by shooting the Federal in the thigh.

To the north of the gap, Manigault's brigade, now reinforced by Colonel Bushrod Jones's Alabama brigade, slammed into the left flank of Charles R. Woods's division, forcing it back.

From high ground near his headquarters less than a mile north of the railroad, Sherman had a clear view through field glasses of the crisis confronting his XV Corps.

"I had never till then seen Sherman with such a look on his face," wrote a Federal officer who saw the commanding general about 4 p.m., at the peak of the crisis. "His eyes flashed. He did not speak. There appeared not only in his face, but in his whole pose, a concentrated fierceness."

Determined to plug the widening gap south of him, Sherman ordered a counterattack by Woods's division. To support them, he ordered Schofield to mass all the guns from his Army of the Ohio — 20 pieces — on a knoll near headquarters. Sherman led the batteries into position and personally sighted the first gun, squinting along the barrel as a stray bullet whizzed past his cheek.

While Sherman mounted this counter-strike, the new commander of the Army of the Tennessee, John Logan, was putting together an attack of his own. Logan was with Dodge's corps at Sugar Creek when an aide informed him XV Corps was in trouble. Logan retrieved a brigade he had lent to Dodge earlier and asked Dodge to let him borrow "the Little Dutchman's brigade."

This brigade, from Sweeny's division, was commanded by German-born Colonel August Mersy. Though Mersy and many of his men were in fact no longer in the U.S. Army — they had been mustered out after their term of service expired — they had volunteered to serve while awaiting transportation home. Now Mersy's four regiments, which already had fought for more than three hours on Dodge's front, turned

Emerging from a shroud of gun smoke, Manigault's Confederate troops swarm over the parapet of De-Gress' battery to claim its four 20-pounder Parrotts. Recalled a Federal artillerist nearby: "Only as the breath of a passing breeze blew the smoke away could the movements of the enemy be discerned clearly; but his unearthly *yell* could be heard above the sound of muskets and cannon."

and headed northward at the double-quick.

Logan himself led them in the mile-and-a-half march to a ravine in the rear of the new Federal line north of the railroad. In all, four divisions were now sending seven brigades to counterattack: Woods's division from the north and west, Morgan L. Smith's and Thomas Sweeny's divisions from the east, and Harrow's division from the south.

As his men formed, the swarthy Logan rode along the lines, waving his broad-brimmed hat and letting his long, jet-black hair stream in the wind. To urge them on, he invoked the memory of his fallen predecessor, shouting over and over again: "McPherson and revenge, boys!"

In return the men chanted their new commander's nickname: "Black Jack! Black Jack! Black Jack!"

Supported by nearly 30 guns firing from north and south, the blue lines converged on the outnumbered Confederates along the railroad. Manigault's and the other Confederate brigades recoiled in shock. "We left in 240 time amidst a shower of grape and canister," wrote Lieutenant R. M. Gill of the 41st Mississippi.

In less than 30 minutes, the Federals had closed the gap and restored XV Corps's original lines, recovering eight of the 10 lost artillery pieces. Mersy's brigade—minus "the Little Dutchman," who had fallen wounded just before the charge—recaptured De-Gress' 20-pounder Parrotts and turned them on the Confederates. DeGress himself arrived and thanked the men profusely even though, in their eagerness, they had loaded one of his prized guns with too great a charge and burst its barrel.

As Cheatham's Confederates retreated, Schofield went to Sherman with a sugges-tion. He proposed to form from his little army and Thomas' big one a strong column to strike Cheatham in flank and roll up the entire Confederate line in front of Atlanta.

But Sherman declined with a smile. "Let the Army of the Tennessee fight it out," he answered. Proud to a fault of his old army, he later explained lamely that he had hesitated to send help because Logan's men "would be jealous."

It was not over yet. As Cheatham retired, Hardee was regrouping south of Bald Hill. Maney's division rallied and moved into position. Cleburne brought up his reserve brigade; several regiments from Walker's division moved west from Sugar Creek.

About 5 p.m., this combined force advanced against the southern flank of Giles Smith's battle-weary division, which already had been pushed back at least 300 yards. Once again, Smith was hit alternately from the south, east and west, and his men had to leap back and forth over their breastworks to meet the enemy. "Every direction," said a Federal officer, "was the front."

The Confederates, their approach often hidden by woods that reached to within 15 yards of the Federal defenses, got so close that sometimes only a breastwork of red clay separated them from the defenders.

"The flags of two opposing regiments would meet on the opposite sides of the same works, and would be flaunted by their respective bearers in each other's faces," reported Giles Smith. "Men were bayoneted across the works, and officers with their swords fought hand-to-hand with men with bayonets."

Colonel Harris D. Lampley's 45th Alabama repeatedly charged the works defended by Colonel William W. Belknap's 15th Iowa. Every time the Iowans repulsed a charge, they would clamber over the breastworks to collect weapons from the dead and wounded Alabamians piling up in front. Their firepower thus replenished, the Iowa men took a heavy toll of their enemy, including three color-bearers shot down in rapid succession.

Undeterred, Lampley attempted to lead his badly depleted regiment in yet another charge. A bullet hit him, but he did not falter. Nearing the breastworks, he turned and started cursing those who had failed to follow. With that, Belknap, the brawny Iowa commander, leaned over the works into a volley of bullets — one ball actually passed through his bushy red beard — and grabbed Lampley by the collar.

He pulled on it, and Lampley fell across the parapet. "Look at your men!" Belknap shouted. "They are all dead! What are you cursing them for?"

Belknap won a brigadier's star for his bravery that day. Lampley died a few days after his capture — more from shame, it was

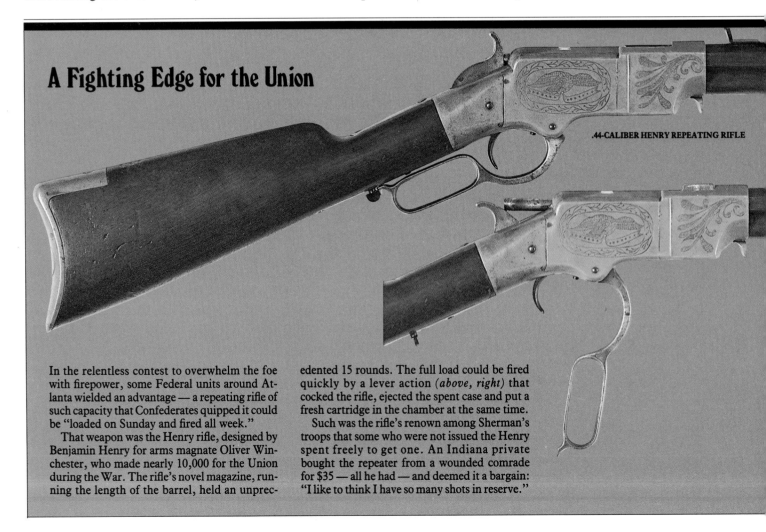

A Fighting Edge for the Union

.44-CALIBER HENRY REPEATING RIFLE

In the relentless contest to overwhelm the foe with firepower, some Federal units around Atlanta wielded an advantage — a repeating rifle of such capacity that Confederates quipped it could be "loaded on Sunday and fired all week."

That weapon was the Henry rifle, designed by Benjamin Henry for arms magnate Oliver Winchester, who made nearly 10,000 for the Union during the War. The rifle's novel magazine, running the length of the barrel, held an unprec-edented 15 rounds. The full load could be fired quickly by a lever action (above, right) that cocked the rifle, ejected the spent case and put a fresh cartridge in the chamber at the same time.

Such was the rifle's renown among Sherman's troops that some who were not issued the Henry spent freely to get one. An Indiana private bought the repeater from a wounded comrade for $35 — all he had — and deemed it a bargain: "I like to think I have so many shots in reserve."

said, than from the wound he suffered in his final charge.

Hardee's Confederates fell back and, at 6 p.m., mounted a final assault. Under fire, Giles Smith managed to pull back northward and form a new, stronger line. Linking with Leggett at Bald Hill, the line extended east toward Sugar Creek to connect with Colonel Hugo Wangelin's brigade of Missourians — the XV Corps reinforcements that McPherson had sought in the last order he ever issued. The new line at last narrowed the gap where McPherson had met his death four hours before, and it proved strong enough to withstand Hardee's final lunge.

There would be no more assaults that day. Cleburne's division, in particular, was spent. Cleburne had lost more than 40 percent of his men in casualties, including 30 of his 60 highest-ranking officers.

After dark, while Cleburne and the remnants of Hardee's left wing clung to their positions south of Bald Hill, the right of Hardee's corps withdrew southward into the dense woods from which they had emerged seven hours before under the bright sun

Posing with their mascot, troops of the 7th Illinois color guard flaunt the rapid-firing Henry rifles that saw them through the Atlanta Campaign.

of noon. The Battle of Atlanta was over.

Hood, despite his anger at what he believed to be Hardee's shortcomings, professed satisfaction with the outcome. "The partial success of that day was productive of much benefit to the army," he wrote. "It greatly improved the *morale* of the troops, infused new life and fresh hopes and demonstrated to the foe our determination not to abandon more territory without at least a manful effort to retain it."

No one questioned that the day's effort had been manful. Hood's casualties on that tumultuous Friday amounted to about 8,000 soldiers, more than double his toll at Peach-

tree Creek two days before. In just five days as commander of the Army of Tennessee, Hood had gambled twice and lost almost as many men as the deposed Johnston had lost in 10 weeks.

In fact, the estimates of Confederate casualties made by Sherman's commanders at Atlanta were so chilling that Sherman at first refused to believe them. His own losses were dreadful enough: a reported 3,722, including 1,733 missing or taken prisoner.

Sherman mourned every loss, but most of all he grieved for McPherson. He remembered with regret that, in the spring, McPherson had asked permission for leave to

In this damaged photograph, the bloated body of a horse lies on the Atlanta battlefield below a fortified hill stripped of its timbers. A witness later wrote of the landscape: "Many trees had fallen by the army-woodman's ax, and those left standing were but the shattered remnants of their former selves. The woods and fields were strewn with the bodies of dead and decaying animals."

marry his fiancée, Emily Hoffman of Baltimore. But Sherman had reluctantly refused because the armies were preparing for the march against Atlanta.

A day or two after the battle, Sherman poured out his heart to Hoffman. "I yield to no one on earth but yourself the right to exceed me in lamentations for our dead hero," he wrote. "Though the cannon booms now, and the angry rattle of musketry tells me that I also will likely pay the same penalty, yet while life lasts I will delight in the memory of that bright particular star which has gone before to prepare the way for us more hardened sinners who must struggle to the end."

By the time Emily Hoffman received that letter, she already knew of her fiancé's death. A telegram had come and a member of the family — strong Southern sympathizers who disapproved of the engagement — read it and exclaimed, "I have the most wonderful news — McPherson is dead!"

Emily heard this and went to her bedroom. She remained there for an entire year in complete seclusion, with curtains drawn, speaking to no one. Like her fallen fiancé — "that bright particular star" — she was a casualty of the Battle of Atlanta.

The Gate City Fortified

As General Sherman's army closed inexorably on Atlanta in the summer of 1864, it faced a forbidding last barrier: the bristling cordon of batteries and rifle pits that ringed the city 12 miles around. In Sherman's words, Atlanta "presented a bold front at all points, with fortified lines that defied a direct assault."

These stout defenses had been a full year in the making. Stung by the loss of Vicksburg the previous summer, the Confederate government had dug deep into its treasury to barricade Atlanta:

The priority, according to chief engineer Lemuel Grant, was "second only to the defense of Richmond." Slaves were hired from their owners at a rate of $25 a month and put to work in droves excavating trenches, raising parapets, and felling trees by the thousands to clear fields of fire and to erect ominously barbed obstructions.

The result was a barrier that inspired profound caution in Sherman's troops and a measure of confidence in the Confederates. "I have heard repeatedly that

the Yankee Gents can't get their men to charge our works," a Texas color-bearer wrote home from Atlanta that August. In fact, Sherman had no intention of risking his forces on such an attack; he would concentrate instead on severing the rail lines feeding the city. This mighty pincers would eventually allow the Federal army to capture the fortifications intact and so enable Union photographer George Barnard to preserve them in the pictures shown here and on the following pages.

On Atlanta's formidable northern perimeter, a sandbagged redoubt for cannon (*lower right*) receives added protection from spiked logs called chevaux-de-frise. Beyond

them a palisade — its timbers spaced to permit riflemen to fire between the slats — snakes past houses whose walls provided lumber for the works.

Behind an earthen rampart, 12-pounder Napoleons stand at embrasures — gaps cut through the wall — in a Confederate bastion now occupied by Federals. Engineers

had bolstered the interior of the works with a revetment, or facing, made of planks and beams and had cleared the land beyond to create an open field of fire.

A 12-pounder looms from Confederate earthworks on a road into Atlanta (*rear*) where Federal engineers are now camped. The embrasure for the cannon was reinforced with sandbags and built with its walls flaring outward to allow the gunners a wider angle of fire.

A Confederate fort on a ridge near Atlanta's Peachtree Street overlooks a long trench for riflemen. The position commands an expanse of open ground over which any attacking infantry would have to come.

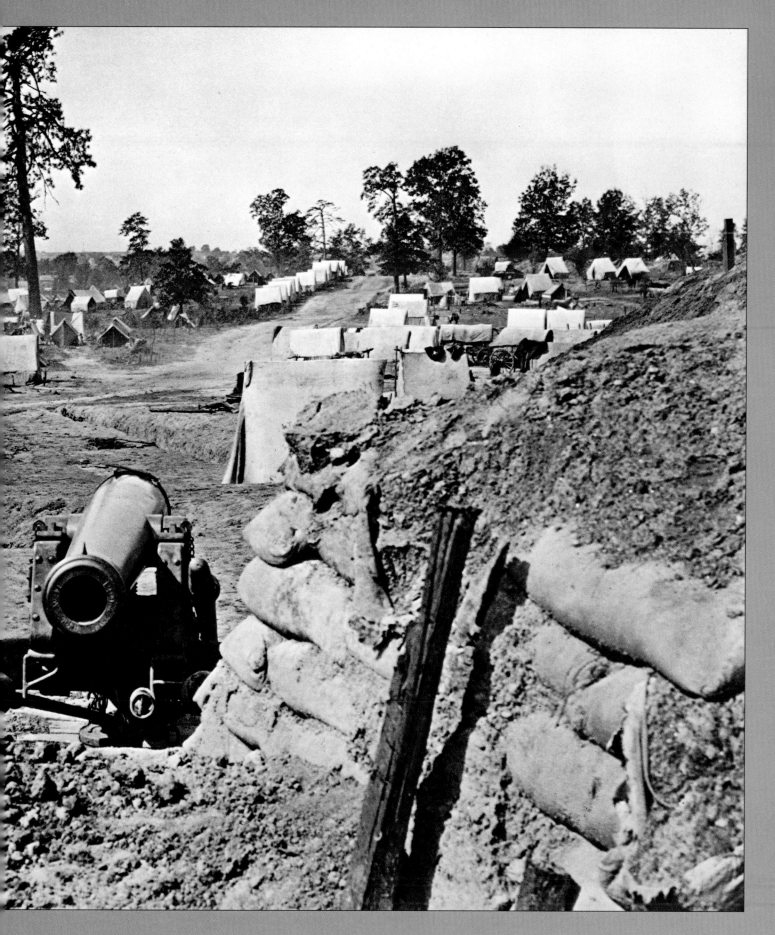

Union soldiers examine a demolished shelter and an abatis — a crude barrier of felled trees — thrown up east of Atlanta by Confederates defending the Georgia Railroad

(rear). **An abandoned locomotive and tender stand idle on the wreckage-strewn tracks.**

The approach to an earthen Confederate fort on Atlanta's Marietta Street is guarded by slanted rows of embedded stakes called fraises, now partially dismantled. Just beyond them are portable spiked logs called chevaux-de-frise. Over these logs "a very meagre man or a small boy might crawl," reported a Union officer, "but not one of our well-fed soldiers with a musket in his hand."

Shaded from the blistering Georgia sun by a roof of planks, a Federal sentry observes a cleared field from his seat on a captured Confederate redoubt. To the hilltop beyond him stretches a palisade, fronted by the sharp stakes of a fraise.

A Federal infantryman surveys the recently contested countryside from an artillery position built by Confederates to defend the Western & Atlantic Railroad.

The soldiers at right have removed a section of chevaux-de-frise from a dirt road to allow passage.

A Confederate rifle pit (*above*) guards the Georgia Railroad east of Atlanta. In front of the trench are so-called head logs — thick timbers set several inches off the ground — that allowed a soldier to fire beneath the logs while providing protection for the man's exposed head. The logs spanning the trench kept the men from being crushed if the head logs were dislodged by artillery fire.

Anticipating a Confederate attempt to retake Atlanta, Union engineers prepared the neatly sculpted trench at left. In contrast to the rough-hewn Confederate works, the logs of the Federal revetment have been sawed to a standard size and the trench itself boasts a double fire step, which a man would climb to fire his weapon, then step down to reload in relative safety.

A Federal soldier reads a book in the casemate of a Confederate-built fort as his comrades lounge about the ramparts. "It is astonishing to see what fortifications they

…ad every side of the city," a Union soldier wrote from Atlanta in the autumn of 1864. "All in vain for them, but quite convenient now for us."

The Circle of Desolation

5 "We have Atlanta close aboard, as the sailors say, but it is a hard nut to handle," William Sherman wrote his wife, Ellen, on July 26, four days after the Battle of Atlanta. "These fellows fight like Devils and Indians combined, and it calls for all my cunning and strength."

Sherman lacked the troops to surround Atlanta and lay siege to the city. And he wisely declined to risk a direct attack against the city's perimeter defenses, which his chief engineer, Captain Orlando M. Poe, described as "too strong to assault and too extensive to invest." Atlanta's impressive fortifications — breastworks and rifle pits studded with a score of fortified batteries — encircled the city at an average distance of a mile and a half from the center.

Instead of testing these defenses, Sherman meant to isolate the city by inscribing around it what he later called "a circle of desolation." His strategy focused on the four railroads that made Atlanta so vital to the South. One route, the Western & Atlantic, Sherman's supply line to Chattanooga, was firmly in Federal control. Another, the Georgia Railroad, running east to Augusta, already had been rendered inoperative by Sherman's rail benders, who had ripped up 30 miles of track. And the third line, the Atlanta & West Point, running southwestward into Alabama, had had about 30 miles of track destroyed during the third week of July by Federal cavalry operating out of Tennessee.

The Confederates in Atlanta possessed only one remaining rail link to the outside world: the Macon & Western Railroad. This line shared a common right-of-way with the Atlanta & West Point track for a five-mile stretch below the city. Then, at East Point, it branched off to the southeast to Macon, 85 miles from Atlanta, making connections there for Savannah and thence Richmond.

To cut the Macon & Western line, Sherman developed a plan for simultaneous movements by cavalry and infantry. Two separate columns of troopers would converge on the line and disrupt it in the vicinity of Lovejoy's Station, about 20 miles southeast of Atlanta. At the same time, from its position just east of the city, the Army of the Tennessee would execute a counterclockwise swing around Atlanta, marching in the rear of the other two Federal armies, then south and east to attack the railroad between the city and East Point.

By thus threatening the Confederates' only line of supply, Sherman hoped to force Hood either to leave his Atlanta fortifications and fight or to evacuate the city altogether.

To lead his old army — his "whiplash" — in this complicated maneuver, Sherman faced the painful and difficult task of finding a permanent replacement for his fallen protégé James McPherson. The senior commander available was Joseph Hooker, but Sherman detested Hooker and never seriously considered him.

MURFREESBORO

LIBERTY GAP   RINGGOLD GAP   PERRY VILLE

6x 7TH A.R.K.
SHILOH
Down with the tyrant.

TUNNEL HILL Tenn

CHICKAMAUGA

This flag of the combined Confederate 6th and 7th Arkansas was captured at bayonet point by Private Henry Mattingly of the 10th Kentucky during the battle at Jonesboro on September 1, 1864. The consolidated regiments had fought through two years of bitter campaigns in Tennessee, Kentucky and Georgia, earning honors for the actions cited on their colors.

The obvious choice was the fiery and charismatic XV Corps commander, John Logan, who had performed so effectively as temporary army commander after McPherson's death. Logan was a politician by trade, however, and not a professional soldier. Moreover, he had once rubbed that paragon of the cautious West Pointers, George Thomas, the wrong way, and Thomas vehemently opposed Logan's appointment.

Even the intuitive Sherman wanted to play it safe in the delicate endeavor ahead. "I wanted to succeed in taking Atlanta," he wrote, "and needed commanders who were purely and technically soldiers, men who would obey orders and execute them promptly and on time."

So Sherman finally settled upon the one-armed commander of IV Corps, Major General Oliver O. Howard. A 33-year-old West Pointer, Howard was an unusual choice to

lead a bunch of high-spirited westerners. He was Logan's — and Sherman's — opposite: a New England abolitionist who never drank, smoked or swore and who was so pious that the troops referred to him as "Old Prayer Book." Perhaps because of these qualities, Sherman considered Howard safe and reliable, despite the latter's blunders in May at Pickett's Mill.

Though deeply hurt at being passed over, Logan nursed his grievances "with the grace and dignity of a soldier, gentleman, and patriot," wrote Sherman. But not Joseph Hooker, who blamed Howard for the Federal defeat the previous year at Chancellorsville — the defeat that had cost Hooker command of the Army of the Potomac.

Citing Howard's selection as an affront to his sense of "justice and self-respect," Hooker asked to be relieved. Sherman granted the request immediately and without regret. Hooker's men were much sorrier to see him go. A Massachusetts soldier wrote that on the day Hooker departed — bound for a desk assignment in Cincinnati — "bronzed old veterans of the corps wept like children."

When Oliver Howard assumed his new command on the morning of Wednesday, July 27, the double strike aimed at the Macon & Western Railroad was already in motion. Cavalry columns were en route south; the Army of the Tennessee had pulled out of its Bald Hill line east of Atlanta and was on the march. By the following morning, Howard's army had completed a half circle around the city. All three corps were now on Thomas' right, a couple of miles west of Atlanta near a little rural chapel known as Ezra Church. From there, Howard could arc south and east toward the railroad.

Unlike Sherman, who thought Hood had shot his wad in the two bloody battles of the past eight days, Howard anticipated trouble. He carefully chose good defensive ground. Grenville Dodge's XVI Corps and Francis Preston Blair's XVII Corps took up a north-south line facing east. On Blair's right, Logan's XV Corps extended the line southward in front of Ezra Church and then bent west at a right angle across the Lickskillet road.

The men piled up temporary breastworks from logs, fence rails and other materials at hand. A group of Logan's Missourians even ventured into the chapel and dragged out pews. These preparations were not wasted, for Howard's premonition proved accurate.

In Atlanta, Hood was fully aware of Howard's march, and he had four divisions from two corps en route to stop it. Hood's old corps — now under the newly arrived Lieutenant General Stephen D. Lee, who replaced the temporary commander, General Cheatham — marched west along the Lickskillet road with orders to block the southward Federal thrust near Ezra Church.

A mile or so behind Lee came Alexander Stewart's corps. Once Lee had stopped the Federal advance, Stewart was to skirt south around Howard's exposed right flank and attack him from the rear.

Late on the morning of July 28, Stephen Lee made contact with Howard's troops. Only 30 years old (the youngest lieutenant general in the Confederacy) and fresh from a cavalry command in Mississippi, Lee was eager to prove his mettle. Without consulting Hood, who as usual remained at headquarters in Atlanta, Lee decided to attack.

He deployed a division under Brigadier General John C. Brown facing northward and launched the troops against the right wing of Logan's corps. A couple of miles away, Sherman heard the opening shots and remarked, "Logan is feeling for them, and I guess he has found them."

Sherman was delighted that his tactics had lured the Confederates out of their Atlanta fortifications. "Just what I wanted," he said gaily when a staff officer reported the assault on Logan. "Tell Howard to invite them to attack, it will save us trouble, save us trouble, they'll only beat their own brains out, beat their own brains out."

In a matter of minutes, it seemed that the

Sheltered by a crude fence, Federals of Logan's XV Corps deliver an enfilading fire on the advancing Confederates near Ezra Church on the afternoon of July 28. The troops were quick to use every barrier at hand. A Union officer on the field that day recalled: "The old-fashioned impression that a soldier should stand up to be shot at had passed away, and he had learned to take what advantage he could of his enemy."

Confederates would do exactly that. One of Brown's brigades lost three commanders in quick succession. In the same brigade, the 25th Alabama took 173 men into battle and lost 125 of them. In front of the 55th Illinois, wrote a member of that regiment, the Confederate dead collected "in windrows, sometimes two or three deep."

Stephen Lee was undeterred. Looking like "the God of War, positively radiant," as one subordinate remembered him, Lee renewed the assault and belatedly sent his other division, under Major General Henry Clayton, against Logan's left wing—but with no better results.

At 2 p.m., Stewart's corps of Confederates arrived on the scene. Stewart, seeing Lee in obvious need of assistance, disregarded his

To defend Atlanta against Federal attack, Confederate engineers ringed the city with a network of elaborate fortifications (red). In places the line was little more than a mile from the center of the city — too close to prevent the Federals from shelling Atlanta at will. During the fighting, the Federals built miles of fieldworks (blue), which traced the course of Sherman's shifting operations.

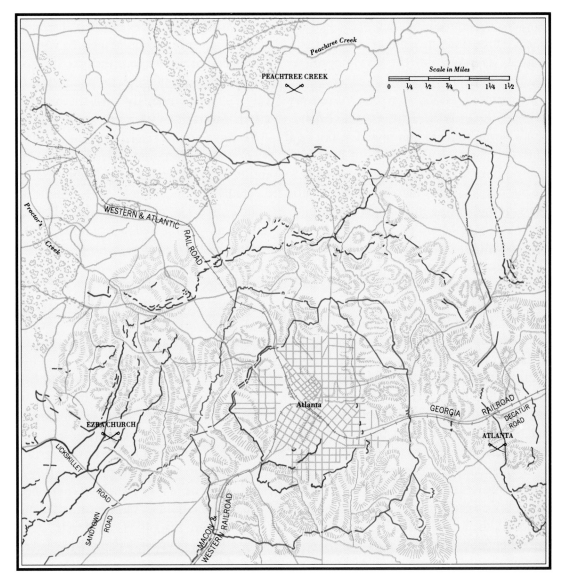

original instructions to wait and flank Howard the following day. He ordered the division under 33-year-old Major General Edward C. Walthall to attack the Union right, where Brown's men had failed.

Walthall formed his men shortly before 3 p.m. Then, riding his dapple-gray horse and brandishing his saber, he led repeated charges against the Federal-held ridge.

His brave perseverance drew the admiration of Colonel William Belknap, whose 15th Iowa had reinforced the right of the Federal line. "Three times he led that grand veteran column, as it were into the jaws of death, to charge upon our works and three times they were repulsed," Belknap wrote. "It seemed as if half the army were firing at the General. I took seven shots at him myself as fast as a musket could be loaded for me. I have seen many mounted officers under fire and in battle but never saw any man bear himself with more heroic daring in the face of death on every side than he did on that day."

Stewart's other division started to deploy for the assault. Then the division commander, Major General William W. Loring, went down severely wounded, and Stewart himself was injured by a ricocheting bullet that hit his forehead.

The intrepid Walthall, who had escaped unhurt, took temporary command of the corps and quickly realized that further assaults would be suicidal. About 5 p.m. he and Stephen Lee withdrew their troops, and the fighting subsided.

Confederate casualties at the Battle of Ezra Church were estimated to be 5,000 killed, wounded or captured. (The Federals, protected by their improvised breastworks, lost only about 600.) In just 10 days under Hood, Confederate losses now exceeded 18,000, or nearly one third of the 60,000-man force available when he took command.

That night near Ezra Church, a Federal picket called out to the Confederate across the way: "Well, Johnny, how many of you are left?"

"Oh," came the answer, "about enough for another killing."

Though Lee's and Stewart's Confederates were badly bloodied, their presence near Ezra Church temporarily blocked Sherman's planned advance on the Macon & Western Railroad. This gave new priority to the Federal cavalry raids that had been launched on July 27 simultaneously with the infantry march toward Ezra Church.

Sherman awaited word from these forays with some trepidation. He distrusted the ability of cavalrymen, with their derring-do tradition, to carry out such prosaic assignments. (The only horseman Sherman respected—and feared—was "that devil," Nathan Bedford Forrest, who thought and fought more like an infantryman than like a trooper.)

The westernmost of the two Federal cavalry columns consisted of 3,500 men under the command of Brigadier General Edward M. McCook. One of the famed "Fighting McCooks," Edward was the 31-year-old first cousin of Daniel McCook Jr., the heroic infantry brigade leader who had fallen a month earlier at Kennesaw Mountain.

McCook's column rode southeastward from the Chattahoochee River and on July 29 came upon one of Hood's wagon trains near Lovejoy's Station. His raiders surprised and captured more than 400 Confederates, then burned 500 wagons and slaughtered nearly 800 mules and horses.

A Death at Ezra Church

GENERAL JOHN M. CORSE

MAJOR THOMAS J. ENNIS

Among the Federals slain at the Battle of Ezra Church was the commander of the 6th Iowa, 23-year-old Major Thomas Jefferson Ennis. The death of this promising officer inspired his close friend, General John M. Corse, to compose a moving and heartfelt tribute. The two had met in 1862 when Ennis, a recent graduate of Hobart College in New York, was appointed adjutant of Corse's regiment. When Corse was promoted to general, he saw to it that Ennis was placed on his staff. Both officers were wounded at Missionary Ridge in November 1863, and they visited each other during their convalescence. Two months after Ezra Church, Corse expressed his deep sense of loss in a poignant letter to Ennis' brother, William. "I felt as if a younger brother who had been under my especial care and protection had fallen," he wrote. The letter, slightly abridged, is below.

I saw Tom the night before his fall. The next day when the battle raged most furiously and success looked dim and distant, Tom was sent with his regiment to stop a column of men sweeping around our right flank. The deeds of that gallant command are now History, their success was the success of the army, but oh how expensive. Tom fell, his face to the enemy and at the head of his spartan band. The most glorious death for a soldier — booted and spurred, sword in hand, big heart and flashing eye, he died in the most sacred cause in which man ever embarked. Although mortally wounded he did not die at once. Shot through the intestines, he lay in painful agony for nearly three hours. When born from the field he asked them to send for me. I stood by my men suffering the agony of this last intelligence and unable to go to him. One hour, two hours and it still hailed iron and rained lead, when suddenly as the rift in the storm blackened heavens, the enemy was hurled back along the entire front and a quiet of death-like character ensued. I waited to hear it was all right on my right when I jumped on my horse and spurred for the hospital where poor Tom lay. He had looked for me long they said, and had fallen into a stupor. The death damp on his brow made me painfully aware how fast he was going. I spoke to him and he immediately turned

and asked, "Is that you General?" — "Dear Tom what *can* I do for you?" — "General, I cling to life with the tenacity of a drowning man to a straw but I know there is no hope for me. Telegraph my brother." He then stopped, evidently not able to see me, his eyes so dazed by death and mist. Then brightening up he said, "Did we whip them?" — I replied that we had repulsed them at every point, punishing them severely. He added the most fervent "Thank God" I ever heard, and that was the last he said. When I reflect on the brave and good that have fallen during this campaign, the young and promising — I am sick at heart. It seems that fate was stricken all my friends, leaving me alone to buffet life, their memories clinging like cerements to my person — impeding my progress and filling me with disgust at a life that spares not the good and true.

I am anxious as all men should be, and I presume are, for a speedy and successful close of this sanguinary feud. I don't question but that our government is worth the life of every man in it — and every man should be ready to lay his down for it. But when I think of the noble that fall and the ignoble that remain to enjoy the boon obtained at such a cost, I am filled with murmurings.

John M. Corse
Brigadier General

McCook was now supposed to rendezvous with the other column of cavalry coming down east of Atlanta under Major General George Stoneman. But there was no sign of Stoneman and his 6,500 troopers. So McCook and his men went to work without the help they had anticipated, burning two trains and ripping up a couple of miles of the Macon & Western.

Starting back, they met the first of five brigades of Joseph Wheeler's Confederate cavalry. The next day, July 30, the Federals were surrounded near Newman, 30 miles southwest of Atlanta, and McCook ordered his units to break out in any direction possible. Over the next few days, remnants of his column straggled back to the Chattahoochee — minus the prisoners taken earlier and minus 600 of their own men, killed or captured. By then, the Confederates had repaired the Macon & Western line.

And what of Stoneman, who had missed his appointed rendezvous with McCook at Lovejoy's Station? Just before Stoneman started out from Decatur, he prevailed upon Sherman to let him undertake an additional mission far more exciting than railroad wrecking. After joining McCook at Lovejoy's Station to cut the Macon & Western, he would ride south to Macon and liberate Union prisoners being held in the jail there; then he would continue 70 miles farther southwest and free the roughly 30,000 Federal captives at the notorious Andersonville camp. Neither Sherman nor Stoneman planned what to do with these sick and weakened prisoners if they were freed, but that seemed no deterrent.

Stoneman realized that such a coup would electrify the North and redeem his own ill-starred reputation. Once a West Pointer of some promise, he was now considered, at the age of 41, a kind of distinguished failure — a reject from the Army of the Potomac, a man whose poor performance at Chancellorsville had contributed to Hooker's defeat there.

In fact, Stoneman was so intent on the glorious possibilities of the second half of his mission that he decided to skip the railroad-wrecking part. Soon after leaving Decatur, he detached Kenner Garrard's 4,000-man division — ostensibly to guard the army's left flank — and then rode straight for Macon with 2,500 troopers.

He reached the east bank of the Ocmulgee River opposite Macon on July 30 — the same day McCook was surrounded. Unable to find a crossing, Stoneman started shelling the town. Armed residents and two regiments of state militia returned the fire.

After an engagement lasting several hours, Stoneman headed back the way he had come. Meanwhile, troopers Stoneman had sent east of Macon torched a couple of railroad bridges and burned 27 cars of a freight train.

Stoneman's cavalry did not get far. Joseph Wheeler had neatly divided his force to deal with both McCook and Stoneman, and he was in hot pursuit. On Sunday, July 31, the Confederate troopers caught up with Stoneman's riders near Clinton, 28 miles northeast of Macon. It was not long before Stoneman concluded that he was surrounded. He ordered two brigades to cut their way out while he staged a last stand with the rest of the division. Those troopers held off the Confederates long enough for the two brigades to escape. Then Stoneman surrendered his remaining 700 men and wound up a prisoner in the Macon jail he had intended to liberate.

The first report of Stoneman's fate came to Sherman on August 4 in the form of a Rich-

mond newspaper sent by Ulysses Grant. After the troopers who had evaded capture straggled in and confirmed the story, Sherman dryly told Washington, "On the whole, the cavalry raid is not deemed a success."

Sherman determined again to try to cut the railroad below Atlanta with his infantry. To do so, he shifted John Schofield's Army of the Ohio counterclockwise from his left flank, northeast of Atlanta, to a position on Howard's right near Utoy Creek, a couple of miles southwest of Ezra Church. On the morning of August 5, Schofield with 12,000 men would spearhead the strike against the Macon & Western Railroad.

Confusion in the Federal command de-layed the operation, however, and Schofield's main attack did not get under way until the morning of August 6. The Federal lapse proved costly; the interval enabled the Confederates to extend their defenses southward. When Schofield moved forward, he found William Bate's division, newly transferred from Atlanta, blocking the way in a strongly entrenched line. In the resulting Battle of Utoy Creek, Schofield lost roughly 300 men before calling off the assault. Although one of Schofield's divisions flanked Bate out of his position late in the afternoon, the Confederates merely fell back to their new line of fortifications at the railroad. Hood was rapidly extending his defenses to East Point, and Sherman decided not to try to outstretch the Confederates to the right. "The enemy can build parapets faster than we can march," Sherman wrote Thomas.

Thwarted again, Sherman turned to his guns, wiring Washington that he intended to "make the inside of Atlanta too hot to be endured." He admitted to Washington that he was "too impatient for a siege." A bombardment would simply satisfy his need to do something while figuring out how best to draw Hood into a decisive battle.

On August 9, Federal gunners poured more than 5,000 shells into the city. On that day at least six civilians, including women and children, died in the bombardment. Sherman had written to his wife of Atlanta that "most of the inhabitants are gone; it is now simply a big fort." But, in fact, about 10,000 civilians remained. Every time the shells started to hiss and shriek, many residents took refuge in their backyard bombproofs — holes dug about 10 feet deep and roofed with planks and several feet of earth.

Hood sent a message to Sherman protesting the bombardment. He cited the thousands of noncombatants still in the city and pointed out that his own defense lines were a full mile from town. Sherman replied that Atlanta was an important military arsenal — and kept up the shelling.

By the third week of August, the struggle for Atlanta had reached a stalemate. Hood had sent Joseph Wheeler and 4,500 cavalrymen northward with orders to sever the Union rail supply line. Wheeler had destroyed several miles of track around Dalton before being driven off; the damage was quickly repaired, but Wheeler stayed on the prowl, sending back sketchy reports of success to Atlanta. Sherman had dispatched Union troopers under Brigadier General Hugh Judson Kilpatrick south to cut the Macon & Western line; their results were negligible. Sherman's right flank was just short of East Point. "Both armies are laying still for the present," Private John Brobst of the 25th Wisconsin wrote his girlfriend, "watching one another to see how and where the other will jump, just like two great savage dogs."

Daily life took on the trappings of trench warfare. Despite orders from Hood that anyone caught fraternizing with the enemy would be shot, Confederates crossed the battle lines to trade tobacco for the Federals' coffee; enemy soldiers even picked blackberries from the same bush. The troops in the trenches engaged in nightly singing duels — the Federals would often lead off with "Yankee Doodle" and the Confederates would respond with "Dixie." The singing typically ended with voices on both sides joining together for "Home, Sweet Home."

But the shelling went on day and night,

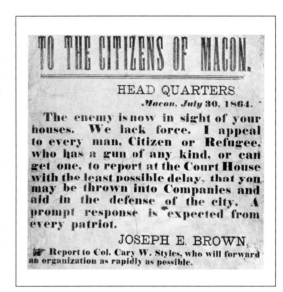

TO THE CITIZENS OF MACON.

HEAD QUARTERS
Macon, July 30, 1864.

The enemy is now in sight of your houses. We lack force. I appeal to every man, Citizen or Refugee, who has a gun of any kind, or can get one, to report at the Court House with the least possible delay, that you may be thrown into Companies and aid in the defense of the city. A prompt response is expected from every patriot.

JOSEPH E. BROWN.

☞ Report to Col. Cary W. Styles, who will forward an organization as rapidly as possible.

An appeal by Georgia Governor Joseph Brown, issued on the day Stoneman's raiders reached the outskirts of Macon, urges civilians to take up arms in the town's defense. Few men in their prime were available to heed the call: Those who came forward were old men, boys and convalescents from Macon's hospitals.

and so did the skirmishing. After sundown, soldiers on both sides placed balls of cotton soaked in turpentine between the lines and set fire to them so that their sharpshooters could pick off anyone who ventured beyond the breastworks.

And the casualties mounted. One day a Confederate marksman spotted the XVI Corps commander, Grenville Dodge, peering through a peephole in the Federal breastworks. The bullet plowed a furrow in Dodge's scalp, sending him North with a painful wound.

These doldrums were hard on the restless Sherman. He detested static warfare and grew irritable and pessimistic. "The enemy hold us by an inferior force," he told Schofield; "we are more besieged than they."

Sherman knew too that this stalemate in Georgia contributed to the growing mood of apathy and discouragement in the North. With General Grant stalled indefinitely in front of Petersburg, the Union's waning hopes fastened on Atlanta. So long as that city held out, the prospects for Lincoln's re-

A guard atop the wall around the teeming Andersonville prison fires on an inmate who has ventured across the picket boundary known aptly as the "dead line." Stoneman's effort to free the 30,000 Federals penned up in this stockade had a galling postscript: Hundreds of his own men were captured and added to its rolls.

election and successful prosecution of the War seemed faint.

No one felt this more acutely than President Lincoln himself. On August 23, Lincoln wrote: "This morning, as for some days past, it seems exceedingly probable that this administration will not be reelected."

That Sherman was the one man in a position to produce a military victory spectacular enough to reelect Lincoln must have struck both men as ironic. Sherman hated politics and had doubts about democracy as well.

But even as the President locked his gloomy prognostication in a desk drawer, the general in Georgia was acting on a plan to break the stalemate. To strangle Hood's life line, he would now cut loose from his own rail supply and march against the Macon & Western with virtually his entire army.

For this hazardous maneuver, Sherman streamlined his force to about 60,000 men. He sent all surplus troops, baggage and wagons back to the Chattahoochee and ordered 20 days' provisions for the march.

The movement began on the night of August 25. While Kenner Garrard's cavalry

dismounted and temporarily occupied the trenches, two corps of Thomas' Army of the Cumberland pulled out of their lines on the northern edge of Atlanta. One of them, XX Corps, marched all the way back to the Chattahoochee to guard the wagon trains and the vital rail bridge over the river. The other, IV Corps, followed partway and then turned south to join with XIV Corps, which was already west of the city with Schofield's Army of the Ohio.

On the next night, Howard's Army of the Tennessee pulled out of its trenches around Ezra Church and moved west toward Sandtown until it came into position facing south on the right of Thomas' troops. These two armies executed a grand left wheel to the southeast, pivoting on Schofield's army, which remained temporarily in position below Utoy Creek and west of East Point.

Thomas and Howard reached the Atlanta & West Point Railroad on the afternoon of August 28 and spent a day and a half tearing up that already disrupted line. For about six miles, stretching from Fairburn northeast toward East Point, they looped the tracks into "Sherman's hairpins" and then added a new twist to their work: All deep cuts traversed by the rails were filled in with trees, soil and live shells that would explode if the enemy tried to remove the debris.

Schofield moved into position across the railroad below East Point to front the Confederate lines there and thus protect the Federal left, or northern, flank. And on the morning of August 30, the armies of Thomas and Howard resumed the advance east toward their main objective, the Macon & Western Railroad. The troops extended along a six-mile front, with Howard on the right and aiming for Jonesboro, about 10 miles distant.

For Sherman, riding with Thomas that Tuesday afternoon, the destruction of the Confederate army was no longer the primary goal. He wanted the city that had eluded his grasp for a month, and now he was confident that it was his. "I have Atlanta," he remarked to Thomas, "as certainly as if it were in my hand."

A slave minds her chores amidst a circle of family members waiting out a bombardment in a sturdy shelter excavated in the garden of an Atlanta home. As the siege wore on, civilians learned to cope with the constant threat of artillery fire. "The shells have been flying all day and we have stayed in the cellar," a 10-year-old girl wrote in her diary that August. "Mama put me on some stockings this morning and I will try to finish them before school commences."

Meanwhile, that battered city had been galvanized by the cessation of the artillery bombardment and the sudden disappearance of the Federal armies.

After Confederate skirmishers found the enemy trenches north of the city abandoned on the morning of August 26, Atlanta's residents poured into the shell-pocked streets to celebrate their apparent good fortune. A victory ball was even scheduled, and trainloads of women steamed up from Macon to join in the festivities. The Federals were gone, and people assumed that Sherman's armies were retreating.

At first, this happy speculation prevailed even in the Confederate high command. Hood and his top generals now thought Wheeler's cavalry had so devastated the Federal supply line that Sherman was pulling back across the Chattahoochee.

Diverse bits of evidence supported their belief. Wheeler was sending back glowing — and inflated — dispatches about his activities. Federal prisoners reported — erroneously — that Confederate cavalry had burned the rail bridge over the Etowah River and destroyed the tunnel at Tunnel Hill.

There were also reports from prisoners and others that Federal rations were running low. An elderly woman who had lived outside Atlanta told William Hardee and Hood she had applied to a Union general for food and been turned down because his soldiers did not have enough. And as if to confirm such stories, Confederate horsemen arrived in Atlanta on August 26 driving a herd of cattle Wheeler had captured from the Federals near Dalton the previous week.

Wheeler's absence prevented Hood from finding out precisely what Sherman was up to. With half the cavalry gone, Hood lacked enough troopers to penetrate the curtain of blueclad cavalry screening the Federal movement west of Atlanta. (And it would be more than a month before Wheeler rejoined Hood; on some wild impulse, the headstrong young cavalry chief had disobeyed orders and pushed into eastern Tennessee.)

On August 28, Confederate scouts reported the presence of Federals on the Atlanta & West Point Railroad below East Point, and Hood became more guarded in his optimism. To protect the Macon & Western line, he ordered two brigades to Jonesboro and moved a division to Rough and Ready, midway between there and Atlanta.

But Hood still did not grasp the magnitude of the threat. He thought the enemy troops might be merely raiding the Atlanta & West Point Railroad as a diversion to cover their withdrawal. He had no idea that practically the entire Federal army was about to march on the Macon & Western.

Not until late afternoon on August 30 — more than four days after Sherman had launched his maneuver — did Hood become aware of the danger. By then, the vanguard of Howard's army was on the east bank of the Flint River, less than two miles from Jonesboro and opposed only by some Confederate cavalry and the two newly arrived brigades of infantry.

At a council of war that night, Hood expressed his belief that the Federal force threatening the railroad consisted of no more than two or three corps — instead of the six Sherman actually had on the march.

To guard the city from the rest of Sherman's army, which he thought was somewhere to the west, Hood would remain in Atlanta with Stewart's corps and the Georgia militia. Hardee would take the other two corps—his and Stephen Lee's—to Jonesboro with orders to attack the Federals and drive them back across the Flint River.

By the following afternoon, the Confederates, 24,000 in all, were deployed on the western edge of town. They outnumbered the Federals facing them on a ridge about a half mile to the west. Oliver Howard had brought only about two thirds of his army— 17,000 men—across the Flint River, leaving the remainder in support on the far bank.

But the Confederates were weary in body —exhausted from their all-night march and from the tedious weeks spent in the trenches of Atlanta. One general, Arthur Manigault, thought his men were not only physically tired but also "dull, sluggish, and entirely without that spirit which had hitherto characterized them."

Once again, they would have to fling themselves against an enemy protected by breastworks: Howard's Federals, watching the Confederates mass that morning at Jonesboro, had taken advantage of the long delay to pile up logs and fence rails and to dig rifle pits. And once again as well, the Confederate assault would be hampered by confusion and a lack of coordination at the top.

Hardee's plan called for his own corps, under Patrick Cleburne, to launch the assault from the left of the line at 3 p.m. The Federal defenses ran north-south, with the right flank bent westward at nearly 90 degrees. Cleburne's three divisions were to oblique to the right in an attempt to turn Howard's southern flank. Stephen Lee was to attack Howard's front as soon as he heard the gunfire signifying that Cleburne was hotly engaged on the left.

But Lee moved too quickly. Mistaking skirmish fire in Cleburne's area for the signal to start, Lee opened the assault at 2:20 p.m.—40 minutes early—sending his three divisions against the front of John Logan's Federal XV Corps.

The premature assault was pressed with vigor by Lee's leftmost division, commanded by Major General James Patton Anderson, a 42-year-old former physician and politician and a well-regarded veteran of the army's earlier campaigns.

Anderson led his men across open terrain to within about 80 yards of the breastworks where Logan's defenders lay in wait. Then the Federals stood up and let loose what Logan called "the most terrible and destructive fire I ever witnessed."

Anderson's grayclads went to the ground and bravely hung on to their position, awaiting reinforcements. But other brigades behind them and farther north moved up haltingly or not at all, balking in the face of such devastating fire. Colonel Bushrod Jones, whose brigade sought shelter behind a rail fence and refused to budge, reported, "The men seemed possessed of some great horror of charging breastworks, which no power, persuasion, or example could dispel."

Patton Anderson, attempting to rally his men for another assault, rode up and down the line in plain view of the Federals, eliciting Logan's unabashed admiration. But Anderson soon went down, twice-wounded. Less than an hour after its premature attack, Lee's corps withdrew, leaving nearly 10 casualties for every one they had inflicted on Logan's defenders.

While Lee was being repulsed, Hardee's corps advanced on the left under Cleburne. The rightmost division, Bate's, now commanded by John C. Brown, charged forward

When General Grenville Dodge was felled by a sniper's bullet outside Atlanta in August, the Union Army lost the services of a capable corps commander and a first-rate engineer: In July, at the Chattahoochee River, he had directed the construction in just two days of a 710-foot-long, double-lane bridge for Sherman's wagon trains. Recovered from his wound, Dodge would help span the continent with rails after the War as chief engineer for the Union Pacific.

and then swung to the right as planned.

The path of attack carried Brown toward the sharp angle in the Union line. Here, the right of XV Corps joined the left of XVI Corps, which bent west to the Flint River.

As the Confederates neared this angle, they ran into trouble. First came a storm of canister from a six-gun battery of 12-pounder Napoleons rapidly firing charges so heavy that three gun trails were broken by the force of the recoils.

Then part of the grayclad line came upon a deep, 10-foot-wide ravine. This gully broke the momentum of the attack not only because it was too wide to jump but also because it provided shelter from the cannon fire. Scores of Confederates took refuge there until the Federals of the 66th Indiana jumped over their breastworks and swept forward to kill or capture practically everyone in the ditch.

On Brown's left, the division of George Maney fared no better coming up in support. "They charged," wrote Private James P. Snell of the 52nd Illinois, "but our boys held their ground, and kept them at bay, with so

little effort that they laughed at the Johnnies — cheered, as they came up — talked with them when they charged our line — and halloed after them as they retired toward their position."

On the far left, Cleburne's division, temporarily commanded by Brigadier General Mark Lowrey, enjoyed the only Confederate success of the day — but a short-lived and hollow one. As Lowrey started to swing north as ordered to hit the Federal right flank, his left suddenly came under fire from an unexpected source — Judson Kilpatrick's cavalry division.

Kilpatrick's dismounted troopers were deployed on the east bank of the river in front of Anthony's Bridge. He had four pieces of artillery, and many of his men were equipped with the much-admired Spencer repeating rifles, which, one Federal officer wrote, "our men adore as the heathen do their idols."

Blazing away from behind piled-up fence rails, the troopers made it so hot for the Confederates that Lowrey was forced to change front to the west to try to eliminate the threat. After a determined fight, Lowrey's division drove the Federal troopers across the bridge. Then, instead of following their commander's orders to turn back to the right and attack the Federal infantry, Lowrey's men went astray. One of the brigades, Hiram Granbury's Texans, persisted in chasing the fleeing enemy cavalry across the river. Close behind the Texans, Lowrey's other two brigades followed suit.

Federal reinforcements finally were able to stop Lowrey's troops in their headlong pursuit and push them back across the river. By that time, the assault by the two other Confederate divisions of Cleburne's corps

had failed. "Nothing, even if I had planned it," wrote the Federal commander, Oliver Howard, "could have been better done to keep an entire Confederate division away from the main battlefield."

Hardee wanted to renew the assault all along the line, but over on the right Lee reported his corps in no condition to attack. His troops had contributed disproportionately to the Confederate casualty list — 1,300 in a total of 1,725 (compared with a reported Federal toll of only 179).

Many of Lee's wounded lay helpless between the lines as the skirmish fire continued in late afternoon. Responding to their cries, Private Sam Chinault of the 54th Virginia jumped over a breastwork and raced onto the

field. Three times he brought back wounded men. The fire was so heavy that one of the soldiers was hit a second time as Chinault carried him to safety.

Farther down the line in Cleburne's area, three Kentuckians from Joseph Lewis' Orphan Brigade took their cue from Chinault and ran forward onto the field. As each of them picked up a wounded comrade and started back, the Federal riflemen across the way stopped shooting and raised a cheer for the gallantry of the rescuers. Then, while Federals actually applauded, the Kentuckians made several more missions of mercy onto the corpse-strewn field.

In Atlanta that evening, John Bell Hood had no information on the Battle of Jones-

Members of a Federal work crew stand beside a self-propelled rail car on a rebuilt trestle bridge over the Chattahoochee River north of Atlanta. The spindly but serviceable structure, bearing the tracks of the vital Western & Atlantic, was erected in the first five days of August by the Railroad Construction Corps after retreating Confederates had burned the original truss bridge. Only the massive brick piers survived that blaze.

boro and little interest in it. He thought the Federal presence there was merely a diversion, and he was preoccupied by what he now perceived to be the principal threat: an attack on Atlanta.

His misconception arose during the afternoon, when the northernmost of the Federal columns cut the Macon & Western Railroad between the city and Jonesboro. Jacob Cox's division from the Army of the Ohio, quickly moving east after protecting the Federal left the day before, reached the tracks a mile below Rough and Ready at 3 p.m. The blue-clads marched north to the station, driving away Confederate cavalry and sending a Confederate supply train steaming in reverse back to Atlanta.

Thus convinced that Sherman intended to assault the city from the south, Hood dispatched a courier to Jonesboro at 6 p.m. without waiting to hear the outcome of the fighting there. He ordered Hardee to remain at Jonesboro — "to protect Macon and communications in rear" — but to send back Lee's corps to help defend Atlanta. (When Hood did learn the result of that day's fighting, he described the Confederate assault as "a disgraceful effort" because the dead and wounded were "a small number in comparison to the forces engaged.")

Lee's corps marched off to the north early Thursday, September 1, taking a detour east of the Federal-held railroad and leaving Hardee holding the army's supply trains — and in deep trouble. Contrary to Hood's notions, not a single Federal column was poised to attack Atlanta. Instead, Sherman's six-corps phalanx was concentrating for a final showdown with Hardee's lone corps at Jonesboro.

Hardee prepared for the worst. Now stripped of nearly half of his command, he stretched his own corps and some cavalry — no more than 13,000 men — in a single line to cover the ground occupied by Lee the previous day and to protect against Howard to the west. Just north of Jonesboro, he angled his right eastward to cross the railroad and guard against the onslaught that he expected from the northwest.

Hardee's men had some time to dig in and build breastworks, thanks to Sherman's leisurely pace that day. Thinking that the Confederates still had two corps at Jonesboro, Sherman kept Howard stationary there and insisted that Thomas and Schofield take the time to thoroughly destroy the railroad as they bore down from the north.

It was nearly 3 p.m. before Sherman learned that Lee's corps had departed Jonesboro — and thus Hardee stood alone. Hurriedly trying to make up for the hours wasted in twisting track, he brought up XIV Corps — now commanded by the aggressive Jefferson C. Davis — to connect with Howard's left north of town near the railroad. And in hopes of striking the Confederate rear, he sent orders for David Stanley's IV Corps — two miles to the north — to stop bending iron and make haste to Jonesboro on the east side of the tracks.

Sherman remarked to Thomas that if Stanley came up in time, the Federals would have Hardee "just like this": In demonstration he enveloped the watch in his hand with fingers and thumb. But Stanley did not ap-

Col. Campbell 13th La

By the time Lieutenant Colonel Francis Campbell led his 13th Louisiana into action at Jonesboro on August 31 — the first day of fighting there — his crack regiment had been so reduced by previous service that it mustered only about 50 battle-weary men. A Confederate general reported that he saw a color-bearer advance with the regiment's flag *(inset)* while "calling upon his comrades to follow. I regret to say that but few responded."

pear; Sherman sent off two staff officers, and then Thomas himself, to hurry him forward. "That is the only time during the campaign," Sherman wrote, "that I can recall seeing General Thomas urge his horse into a gallop."

Unable to wait for Stanley, Sherman ordered Davis' corps to attack the northern part of the Confederate line. About 4 p.m. Davis launched two brigades in a preliminary action, which was quickly repulsed. He then brought up the bulk of his three divisions and, shortly before 5 p.m., ordered a full assault across a cotton field.

The attack centered on the angle where the Confederate line turned back to the rail-

road. As the Federals moved forward on either side of this salient, they came under intense shelling and then blasts of double canister from two Confederate batteries posted near the angle.

Davis' men fell by the score. On the Federal right, a volley of canister fired from a range of only 20 yards blew a huge hole in the ranks of the 78th Illinois. In the center, in front of the angle, one of Major General Absalom Baird's brigades lost one third of its men in just a few minutes. Baird himself had two horses shot from under him as he rode at the head of his division.

"There was no chance for flinching there," remembered Baird's aide, Major James Connolly. "Generals, Colonels, Majors, Captains and privates, all had to go forward together over that open field, facing and drawing nearer to death at every step we took, our horses crazy, frantic with the howling of shells, the rattling of canister and the whistling of bullets, ourselves delirious with the wild excitement of the moment, and thinking only of getting over those breastworks."

Braving canister and bullets, Union soldiers rushed into the Confederate defenses with bayonets at the ready. In Baird's 10th Kentucky Regiment, three brothers named Noe climbed over the parapet together — and two of them pinned Confederates to the ground with their bayonets. Baird reported afterward, "On no occasion within my knowledge has the use of the bayonet been so general or so well authenticated."

On both sides of the angle, men in blue and gray came face-to-face in mortal combat. Two color-bearers from the 17th New York stormed into the rifle pits near the salient and began beating the defenders over the head with their flagstaffs. A pair of Arkansans from Daniel Govan's brigade rose up and ran them through with bayonets.

Farther to the Confederate right, Lewis' Orphan Brigade of Kentuckians held their ground with the same ferocity. A Federal jumped up on the parapet and shouted to Private Booker Reed, "Surrender, you damn rebels."

"The hell you say," responded Reed, and then shot him dead.

Sergeant Major Johnny Green of the 16th Kentucky looked over the parapet to see "a yankee with the muzzle of his gun not six inches from my face." The blast knocked Green down but wounded him only slightly. "I rose and put my gun against his side," wrote Green, "and shot a hole through him big enough to have run my fist through."

But at the angle and farther left, Govan's brigade began to give way. And the two Confederate batteries — already so riddled by enemy artillery fire that several of the gun carriages lay on the ground in splinters — were overwhelmed by the onrushing Federals, who captured all eight pieces.

Govan's infantry fought on with clubbed guns and bayonets. In a short time, however, these Arkansans succumbed to the mass of attackers. "They ran over us like a drove of Texas beeves, by sheer force of num-bers," recalled Private Stan C. Harvey.

About 600 members of the brigade were forced to surrender, including Govan himself. Govan's capitulation opened a wide gap to the left of the angle. Federals swarmed through to threaten the rear of Lewis' Kentuckians on their left and Granbury's Texas Brigade on their right.

But both Confederate brigades managed to fall back in good order, and with the help of reinforcements and massed artillery, they created a new defensive line. The new line held until darkness stopped the fighting around Jonesboro.

In a sketch made during the Battle of Jonesboro on September 1 by soldier-artist Henry Dwight, a Federal artilleryman rams home a round on one gun as a batterymate pulls the lanyard on the other. The cannon fire caught the Confederates as they were building entrenchments against an assault by Jefferson Davis' infantry, seen advancing at far left. "We dug for dear life," one of the defenders wrote. "The yanks began to shell us but we could not stop."

On the afternoon of September 1, Davis' XIV Corps attacked Hardee's Confederates along the Macon & Western Railroad north of Jonesboro. Major John Edie's brigade, in the lead, faltered at the salient formed by the junction of Lewis' and Govan's Confederate brigades. The Federals then launched a three-pronged assault: As divisions under William Carlin and James D. Morgan advanced on either flank, Absalom Baird's division charged the salient with bayonets fixed, breaking through and capturing hundreds of Govan's men. The remaining Confederates managed an orderly retreat, but Atlanta's fate was sealed.

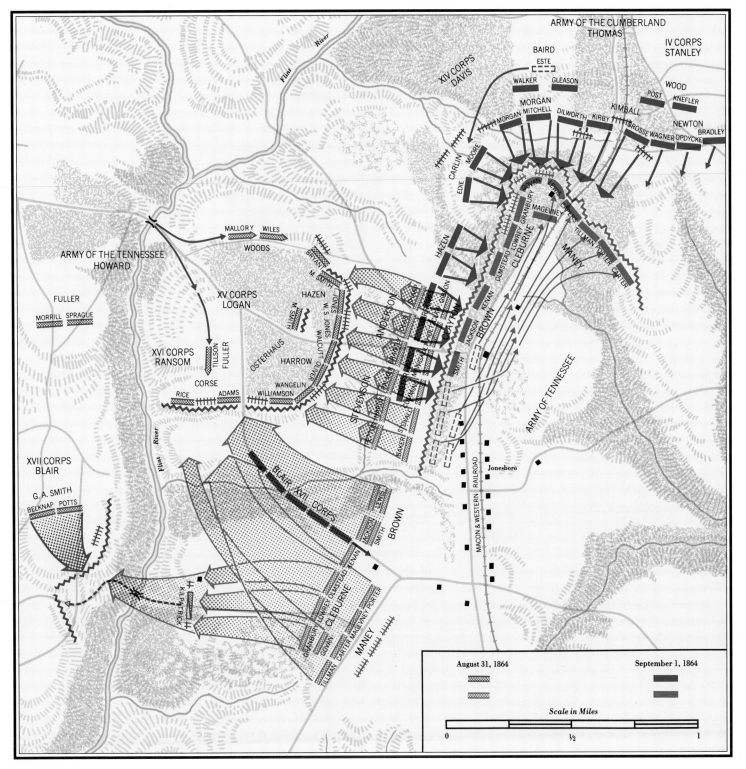

Sherman's assault with a single corps cost him nearly 1,300 casualties and the opportunity to trap Hardee. The Federal IV Corps, getting tangled up in the woods after a slow start, deployed east of the railroad too late to join the fray. Though Sherman privately faulted David Stanley's tardiness, his own obsession with tearing up the railroad contributed to the delay.

And Sherman had only himself to blame for failing to seal off the area south of Jonesboro. Too late in the day, he sent Blair's XVII Corps marching there from Howard's army, and Blair was able to move only a couple of miles before night ended his advance.

Given this welcome reprieve, Hardee began withdrawing his battered units from the Jonesboro lines shortly before midnight. Among the troops were the remnants of three of the best and proudest brigades in the Confederate Army: Lewis', Govan's and Granbury's. Lewis' Orphans, who had started the campaign with 1,500 men, could now count scarcely one third that number, and the great majority of these survivors had been wounded, some twice. As for Govan's brigade, the day's surrender had so mortified the handful of survivors that, on the following morning, a delegation of Arkansans would go to Granbury's men seeking reassurance that the Texans had not lost confidence in them.

Hardee formed his columns to face south, away from Atlanta. Then, slipping out of Sherman's noose, they started the retreat to Lovejoy's Station, six miles farther down the Macon & Western Railroad.

Hardee's were not the only Confederate soldiers marching south that night.

Earlier on Thursday, Hood finally had re-

An Arkansas planter before the War, Brigadier General Daniel Govan was among those captured at Jonesboro on September 1. Exchanged before the year was out, he served the Confederacy until the bitter end, surrendering with Joseph Johnston in North Carolina in April 1865.

alized the extent of the Federal threat and had ordered the evacuation of Atlanta. At 5 p.m. — just as Hardee braced for the Federal assault at Jonesboro — Stewart's corps began the withdrawal. Sad-faced and weary, the men marched south toward McDonough, singing the mournful ballad "Lorena," whose lyrics spoke of happier days: " 'Twas flow'ry May, / When up the hilly slope we climbed . . ."

Lee's corps, which had been heading toward Atlanta, was stopped short and diverted east to McDonough. From there, all would reunite with Hardee at Lovejoy's Station, 10 miles to the west.

The only Confederates still in Atlanta were rearguard cavalry. Just after midnight, on September 2, these troopers set fire to the army's reserve ordnance train and other valuable matériel that the chief quartermaster — rumored to be "too much addicted to drink of late to attend to his duties," according to Hood — had neglected to send to safety while the railroad was still operating.

Five locomotives, 81 rail cars, 13 siege guns, countless shells — all went up in an in-

A Georgia woman offers a drink to a man in a column of Confederate prisoners being led to Union-held Atlanta after the Battle of Jonesboro. A prisoner recalled that the Federals promised freedom to those who would pledge loyalty to the Union: "But thank God not one of our brigade would listen to them."

ferno that continued to blaze for more than five hours and shook the earth for miles around. To Wallace Reed, one of the few thousand civilians remaining in Atlanta that night, it was "more terrible than the greatest battle ever fought."

Sherman, at Jonesboro, heard the explosions; he suspected the truth but could not be certain. Earlier, he had sent orders for Major General Henry Slocum, new commander of XX Corps, guarding the railroad bridge at the Chattahoochee, to probe toward Atlanta. It was possible, Sherman realized, that Slocum had provoked Hood into a mighty battle.

Slocum also heard the sounds from his camp northwest of Atlanta, but he knew exactly what they meant. In the morning — while Sherman, still in doubt, pursued Hardee south to Lovejoy's Station — Slocum marched on Atlanta.

On the outskirts of the city, near an abandoned Confederate redoubt known as Fort Hood, Slocum's lead column encountered a mounted group of well-dressed civilians flying a flag of truce. It was a delegation of prominent residents, led by the Mayor of Atlanta, James M. Calhoun, riding out in search of General Sherman.

Mayor Calhoun consulted with the senior Federal officer present, Colonel John Coburn of the 33rd Indiana. Then, at 11 a.m., Calhoun wrote out a brief note, formally surrendering the city on September 2 and asking protection for "non-combatants and private property."

Rumors of the surrender moved faster than the courier that Slocum dispatched to Sherman. But Sherman—waiting at his headquarters near Lovejoy's Station—could not be certain until the courier arrived after midnight with Slocum's handwritten note dated inside Atlanta. Sherman recalled that when he showed the note to Thomas, that stout general "snapped his fingers, whistled, and almost danced."

At 6 a.m. on Saturday, September 3, Sherman wired Washington a summary of recent operations and added a trenchant line: "So Atlanta is ours, and fairly won."

The news sent the Union into a frenzy of celebration. Sherman's accomplishment was thereby significant in more ways than one: By capturing the city of Atlanta, his armies had not only deprived the Confederacy of a vital arsenal and rail hub, but they had strengthened the will for the Union to continue the War as well.

President Lincoln, whose reelection was now virtually assured, proclaimed a national day of thanksgiving and ordered the firing of 100-gun salutes in more than a dozen cities. Ulysses Grant, from the stalemated Federal line at Petersburg, wrote his old partner, "You have accomplished the most gigantic undertaking given to any general in this war, and with a skill and ability that will be

acknowledged in history as unsurpassed if not unequaled."

Sherman had failed in his primary objective of destroying the Confederate army, but he was satisfied, content to probe halfheartedly for a couple of days more at Lovejoy's Station, where Hood now had concentrated his entire army.

Then, on September 5, Sherman began withdrawing north toward Atlanta, ending the campaign he had launched from Chattanooga four months before. After 128 days

Severed tracks and scattered axles testify to the force of the explosions that ripped through a Confederate ordnance train loaded with shells on the night of September 1, leveling the walls of the plant in the background. Touched off by Hood's men as they prepared to abandon Atlanta to the Federals, the blasts left a path of devastation a half mile wide in this evacuated area and cloaked the city with a pall of sulfurous fumes.

of almost-constant fighting, and at a toll of 35,000 casualties in the Confederate army and nearly as many in their own, Sherman's men would rest.

Not until three days later did Sherman set foot in the conquered city. His entrance was typically low-keyed. Dressed as usual in his gray flannel shirt and shabby blue tunic and trousers, he rode without fanfare to his new headquarters near the courthouse square.

Anxious citizens peered from doors and windows, hoping to catch a glimpse of the conqueror of Atlanta. A reporter from New York noted that "there was not even a shout or huzza to welcome him."

The pall of gloom had spread outward from Atlanta. About 200 miles to the east, in Columbia, South Carolina, the diarist Mary Boykin Chesnut, a volunteer nurse, summed up the despair of Southerners everywhere: "Atlanta is gone. That agony is over. There is no hope, but we will try to have no fear."

"Atlanta is Ours!"

After a night alive with the infernal sounds of warfare, a seemingly endless column of Federal soldiers marched down Atlanta's Marietta Street at midday on September 2, 1864, to take possession of the city. "The long agony is over," wrote Major James Connolly of the 123rd Illinois, "and Atlanta is ours!"

For General Sherman, the victory was only the beginning of a campaign that he predicted would sound the "death-knell of the Southern Confederacy." But for the moment, the occupation of Atlanta afforded his troops a much-needed period of rest. The Federals settled in — officers taking over residences, enlisted men erecting barracks and tent cities. Many of the Federals were shocked by the devastation wreaked by their long siege. Once-proud homes lay in ruins, and scores of famished citizens wandered through the streets.

For some of the beleaguered Atlantans the Union victory brought something approaching relief. Many of the homeless, sick and hungry received sympathetic attention from Sherman's men, and for the time being at least, the destruction of their city had ceased. Other residents were not even aware that the city had changed hands until the occupation came to their doorsteps. One woman, upon seeing two men rummaging through her garden, ran toward them crying, "You scamps! You're worse than the Yanks!"

"Madam," one of the men replied, "we are the Yanks."

Men of the 2nd Massachusetts bivouac in Atlanta's main square, directly in front of city hall. The planks and windows used to construct their canvas-covered huts were scavenged from nearby buildings.

A color sergeant named Johnson of
the 2nd Massachusetts has his picture taken holding his regiment's flag
on the steps of Atlanta's courthouse.
When the Stars and Stripes were
raised over the building, wrote one
observer, "such a cheer went up as
only a conquering army, flushed
with victory, can give."

Staff officers of the Federal XX Corps meet in front of the house that only a few days earlier had been Confederate General Hood's headquarters. Union flags, such as the one draped festively over the front door, appeared all over the city, though some bold Atlantans still flew their Confederate Stars and Bars.

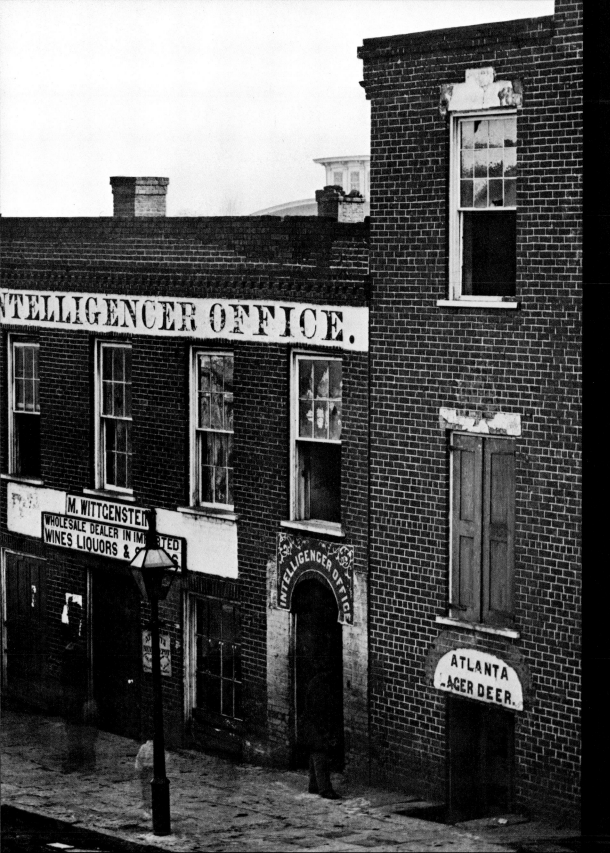

At Atlanta's railroad depot, Federal soldiers crowd the roofs of boxcars on the newly rebuilt line that connected Atlanta with Union-held Chattanooga. The station, located next to the Atlanta *Intelligencer* newspaper office, had been the center of rail transport for the Deep South.

Near Atlanta's railroad yard, a covered military caravan rolls past civilian wagons loaded with hastily gathered possessions. Alongside the arc-roofed car

The Bereaved City

The occupation was less than a week old when a grim public notice was posted around Atlanta ordering all citizens to evacuate the city. The exodus was a bitter one, as families who had endured the siege were forced to give up their homes. Those few Atlantans who evaded the evacuation order would bear witness to an even more somber event: In several weeks, Sherman would put much of Atlanta to the torch.

A lone Union sentry sits outside an abandoned slave market on a deserted street in Atlanta's business district. "Our Negro property," lamented one resident in his diary, "has all vanished into air."

shed at rear, a last trainload of refugees prepares to leave the city.

Shell-wracked homes (*below*) were familiar sights in Atlanta — in ruins by autumn 1864. Sherman wrote to Hood, upbraiding the Confederate general for defending the city "on a line so close to town that every cannon shot and many musket shots from our line of investment, that overshot their mark, went into the habitations of women and children."

Chimneys are all that remain of a
building near the tracks after Sherman burned much of Atlanta in mid-
November. "We have been utterly
destroying everything in the city of
any use to the armies of the South,"
an Indiana soldier wrote. "General
Sherman is credited with saying 'War
is Hell,' I think that it is."

A bank office at the intersection of Peachtree Street and the tracks of the Georgia Railroad was among those buildings destroyed when Sherman's men ravaged

Atlanta's business district. All of the city's banks were shut down during the Federal occupation; few of them ever reopened.

A demolition squad pries loose a section of track in Atlanta's rail yard. Adhering to Sherman's order that "the destruction be so thorough that not a rail or tie can be used again," the Federals heated the rails red-hot over burning ties, then twisted them out of shape. The twisted rails became known as "Sherman's hairpins."

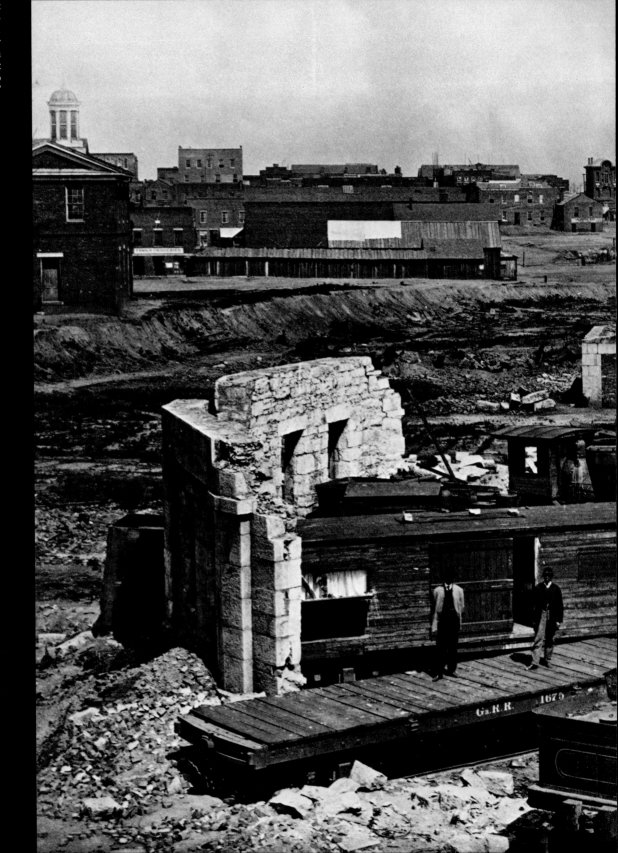

Locomotives and freight cars stand isolated in the ruins of Atlanta's roundhouse. The devastation of the city was so widespread, a Union private wrote, "that I don't think any people will want to try and live there now."

ACKNOWLEDGMENTS

The editors wish to thank the following individuals and institutions for their valuable assistance in the preparation of this volume:

Georgia: Atlanta — Franklin Garrett, Elaine Kirkland, Nancy Wight, Atlanta Historical Society. Marietta — Dennis Kelly, Kennesaw Mountain National Battlefield Park. Roswell — Michael Hitt.

Indiana: Elkhart — Betty Foster Strauss.

Kentucky: Lewisburg — Milton Bates.

Louisiana: New Orleans — Pat Eymard, Confederate Memorial Hall.

New York: Delhi — Herbert Sorgen, State University of New York. Lyons — Charles E. Ennis. Nanuet — Richard Ricca. New York — Gustav Berger, Mira Berger, Berger Art Conservation Inc. Oneonta — James Milne Library, State University College of New York. West Point — Elaine Eatrosf, West Point Library.

Ohio: Columbus — Tauni Graham, Ohio Historical Society; L. M. Strayer.

Pennsylvania: Carlisle — Randy Hackenburg, Michael J. Winey, U.S. Army Military History Institute. Harrisburg — Richard A. Sauers, Pennsylvania Capitol Preservation Com-

mittee. Philadelphia — J. Britt McCarley, Temple University.

Tennessee: Murfreesboro — Daniel Brown, Stones River National Battlefield.

Virginia: Falls Church — Chris Nelson.

Washington, D.C.: Barbara Burger, Deborah Edge and staff, Still Pictures Branch, National Archives; Eveline Nave, Photoduplication Service, Library of Congress.

Wisconsin: Milwaukee — Charles W. Cooney Jr., Milwaukee County Historical Society.

The index for this book was prepared by Roy Nanovic.

BIBLIOGRAPHY

Books

Anders, Leslie, *The Eighteenth Missouri.* Indianapolis: Bobbs-Merrill, 1968.

Andrews, J. Cutler, *The South Reports the Civil War.* Princeton, N.J.: Princeton University Press, 1970.

Barker, Ren, *Birge's Western Sharpshooters in the Civil War.* Reed City, Mich.: Privately published, 1905.

Barnard, George N., *Photographic Views of Sherman's Campaign.* New York: Dover Publications, 1977.

Barnes, James A., *The Eighty-Sixth Regiment, Indiana Volunteer Infantry.* Crawfordsville, Ind.: The Journal Co., 1895.

Belknap, William Worth, *History of the Fifteenth Regiment, Iowa Veteran Volunteer Infantry.* Keokuk, Iowa: R. B. Ogden & Son, 1887.

Benton, Charles Edward, *As Seen from the Ranks: A Boy in the Civil War.* New York: G. P. Putnam's Sons, 1902.

Bierce, Ambrose, *The Collected Works of Ambrose Bierce.* Vol. 1. New York: Gordian Press, 1966.

Black, Robert C., III, *The Railroads of the Confederacy.* Chapel Hill: University of North Carolina Press, 1952.

Boyle, John Richards, *Soldiers True: The Story of the One Hundred and Eleventh Regiment Pennsylvania Veteran Volunteers.* New York: Eaton & Mains, 1903.

Brock, R. A., ed., *Southern Historical Society Papers.* Millwood, N.Y.: Kraus Reprint Co., 1977 (reprint of 1896 edition).

Brown, Joseph M., *The Mountain Campaigns in Georgia.* Buffalo: Matthews, Northrup & Co., 1890.

Bryan, T. Conn, *Confederate Georgia.* Athens: University of Georgia Press, 1953.

Buck, Irving A., *Cleburne and His Command.* Dayton: Morningside Bookshop, 1982.

Bull, Rice C., *Soldiering: The Civil War Diary of Rice C. Bull, 123rd New York Volunteer Infantry.* Ed. by K. Jack Bauer. San Rafael, Calif.: Presidio Press, 1977.

Carpenter, John Alcott, *Sword and Olive Branch: Oliver Otis Howard.* Pittsburgh: University of Pittsburgh Press, 1964.

Carter, Samuel, III, *The Siege of Atlanta, 1864.* New York: Ballantine Books, 1973.

Catton, Bruce:
    Never Call Retreat. Vol. 3 of *The Centennial History of the Civil War.* Garden City, N.Y.: Doubleday, 1965.
    This Hallowed Ground. New York: Pocket Books, 1961.

Chamberlin, William Henry, *History of the Eighty-First Regiment Ohio Infantry Volunteers, during the War of the Rebellion.* Cincinnati: Gazette Steam Printing House, 1865.

Clark, Charles T., *Opdycke Tigers: 125th O.V.I.* Columbus, Ohio: Spahr & Glenn, 1895.

Cleaves, Freeman, *Rock of Chickamauga.* Norman: University of Oklahoma Press, 1949.

Connolly, Thomas Lawrence, *Autumn of Glory: The Army of

Tennessee, 1862-1865.* Baton Rouge: Louisiana State University Press, 1971.

Connolly, James A., *Three Years in the Army of the Cumberland.* Ed. by Paul M. Angle. Bloomington: Indiana University Press, 1959.

Conyngham, David Power, *Sherman's March through the South.* New York: Sheldon and Co., 1865.

Cope, Alexis, *The Fifteenth Ohio Volunteers and Its Campaigns: War of 1861-5.* Columbus, Ohio: Privately published, 1916.

Cox, Jacob D., *Atlanta.* New York: Charles Scribner's Sons, 1882.

Davis, William C., ed., *The End of an Era.* Vol. 6 of *The Image of War, 1861-1865.* Garden City, N.Y.: Doubleday, 1984.

Dodge, Grenville M., *The Battle of Atlanta and Other Campaigns, Addresses, etc.* Council Bluffs, Iowa: Monarch Printing Co., 1910.

Duke, John K., *History of the Fifty-Third Regiment Ohio Volunteer Infantry, during the War of the Rebellion 1861-1865.* Portsmouth, Ohio: The Blade Printing Co., 1900.

Dyer, John P., *"Fightin' Joe" Wheeler.* University, La.: Louisiana State University Press, 1941.

Edwards, William B., *Civil War Guns.* Secaucus, N.J.: Castle Books, 1962.

Fatout, Paul, *Ambrose Bierce: The Devil's Lexicographer.* Norman: University of Oklahoma Press, 1951.

Foote, Shelby, *The Civil War, a Narrative: Red River to Appomattox.* New York: Random House, 1974.

Foster, Samuel T., *One of Cleburne's Command: The Civil War Reminiscences and Diary of Capt. Samuel T. Foster.* Ed. by Norman D. Brown. Austin: University of Texas Press, 1980.

Garfield, James A., *The Wild Life of the Army: Civil War Letters of James A. Garfield.* Ed. by Frederick D. Williams. East Lansing: Michigan State University Press, 1964.

Govan, Gilbert E., and James W. Livingood, *A Different Valor: The Story of General Joseph E. Johnston, C.S.A.* New York: Bobbs-Merrill Co., 1956.

Green, Johnny, *Johnny Green of the Orphan Brigade.* Ed. by A. D. Kirwan. Lexington: University of Kentucky Press, 1956.

Hay, Thomas Robson, ed., *Pat Cleburne: Stonewall Jackson of the West.* Dayton: Morningside Bookshop, 1982.

Hazen, William Babcock, *A Narrative of Military Service.* Boston: Ticknor and Co., 1885.

Hedley, F. Y., *Marching through Georgia.* Chicago: Donohue, Henneberry & Co., 1890.

Hicken, Victor, *Illinois in the Civil War.* Urbana: University of Illinois Press, 1966.

Hitchcock, Henry, *Marching with Sherman.* Ed. by M. A. DeWolfe Howe. New Haven, Conn.: Yale University Press, 1927.

Hoehling, A. A., *Last Train from Atlanta.* New York: Thomas Yoseloff, 1958.

Hood, J. B., *Advance and Retreat.* Ed. by Richard N. Current. Bloomington: Indiana University Press, 1959.

Horn, Stanley F., *The Army of Tennessee.* Norman: University of Oklahoma Press, 1952.

Howard, Oliver Otis, *Autobiography of Oliver Otis Howard: Major General United States Army.* Vol. 2. Freeport, N.Y.: Books for Libraries Press, 1971 (reprint of 1907 edition).

Howe, Mark DeWolfe, ed., *Home Letters of General Sherman.* New York: Scribner's, 1909.

Hughes, Nathaniel Cheairs, Jr., *General William J. Hardee.* Baton Rouge: Louisiana State University Press, 1965.

Johnson, Robert Underwood, and Clarence Clough Buel, *Battles and Leaders of the Civil War.* Vol. 4. New York: Thomas Yoseloff, 1956.

Johnston, Isaac N., *Four Months in Libby, and the Campaign against Atlanta.* Cincinnati: Methodist Book Concern, 1864.

Johnston, Joseph E., *Narrative of Military Operations.* Bloomington: Indiana University Press, 1959.

Joyce, John Alexander, *A Checkered Life.* Chicago: S. P. Rounds Jr., 1883.

Kerksis, Sydney C., comp., and Lee A. Wallace Jr., *The Atlanta Papers.* Dayton: Morningside Bookshop, 1980.

Key, William, *The Battle of Atlanta and the Georgia Campaign.* Atlanta: Peachtree Publishers, Ltd., 1981.

Kurtz, Wilbur G., *Atlanta and the Old South: Paintings and Drawings.* Atlanta: American Lithograph Co., 1969.

Lewis, Lloyd, *Sherman: Fighting Prophet.* New York: Harcourt, Brace and Co., 1932.

Liddell Hart, B. H., *Sherman: Soldier, Realist, American.* Westport, Conn.: Greenwood Press, 1978.

Lucas, D. R., *History of the 99th Indiana Infantry.* Lafayette, Ind.: Rosser & Spring, 1865.

McDonough, James L., *Schofield.* Tallahassee: Florida State University Press, 1972.

McMurry, Richard M., *John Bell Hood and the War for Southern Independence.* Lexington: University Press of Kentucky, 1982.

Manigault, Arthur Middleton, *A Carolinian Goes to War.* Ed. by R. Lockwood Tower. Columbia: University of South Carolina Press, 1983.

Marszalek, John F., *Sherman's Other War.* Memphis: Memphis State University Press, 1981.

Mathews, Byron H., Jr., *The McCook-Stoneman Raid.* Philadelphia: Dorrance & Co., 1976.

Merrill, James M., *William Tecumseh Sherman.* New York: Rand McNally & Co., 1971.

Merrill, Samuel, *The Seventieth Indiana Volunteer Infantry in the War of the Rebellion.* Indianapolis: Bowen-Merrill Co.,

1900.

Morhous, Henry C., *Reminiscences of the 123d Regiment, N.Y.S.V.* Greenwich, Conn.: People's Journal Book and Job Office, 1879.

Nichols, George Ward, *The Story of the Great March.* New York: Harper & Brothers, 1865.

Nisbet, James Cooper, *4 Years on the Firing Line.* Ed. by Bell Irvin Wiley. Jackson, Tenn.: McCowat-Mercer Press, 1963.

Richardson, Eldon B., *Kolb's Farm: Rehearsal for Atlanta's Doom.* Privately published, 1979.

Ridley, Bromfield Lewis, *Battles and Sketches of the Army of the Tennessee.* Mexico, Mo.: Missouri Printing, 1906.

Saunier, Joseph A., ed., *A History of the Forty-Seventh Regiment, Ohio Veteran Volunteer Infantry, Army of the Tennessee.* Hillsboro, Ohio: Lyle Printing Co., 1903.

Seitz, Don C., *Braxton Bragg: General of the Confederacy.* Columbia, S.C.: The State Co., 1924.

Sherman, William T., *Memoirs of General William T. Sherman.* Westport, Conn.: Greenwood Press, 1957.

Sievers, Harry J., *Benjamin Harrison: Hoosier Warrior.* New York: University Publishers, 1960.

Stanley, David Sloane, *Personal Memoirs of Major-General David Sloane Stanley, U.S.A.* Cambridge: Harvard University Press, 1917.

Thomas, Henry W., *History of the Doles-Cook Brigade.* Atlanta: Franklin Printing, 1903.

United States War Department, *War of the Rebellion: A Compilation of the Official Records of the Union and Confederate Armies.* Series 1: Vol. 38, Parts 1-5 and *Additions and Corrections.* Washington: GPO, 1891-1902.

Upson, Theodore F., *With Sherman to the Sea.* Ed. by Oscar Osburn Winther. Baton Rouge: Louisiana State University Press, 1943.

Watkins, Sam R., *"Co. Aytch": A Side Show of the Big Show.* New York: Collier Books, 1962.

Wheeler, Richard, *Sherman's March.* New York: Thomas Y. Crowell, 1978.

Williams, Alpheus S., *From the Cannon's Mouth.* Ed. by Milo M. Quaife. Detroit: Wayne State University Press, 1959.

Williams, T. Harry, *McClellan, Sherman and Grant.* New Brunswick, N.J.: Rutgers University Press, 1962.

Wright, Charles, *A Corporal's Story: Experiences in the Ranks of Company C, 81st Ohio Vol. Infantry.* Philadelphia: Privately published, 1887.

Wright, Henry H., *A History of the Sixth Iowa Infantry.* Iowa City: State Historical Society of Iowa, 1923.

Wyeth, John A., *Life of General Nathan Bedford Forrest.* Dayton: Morningside Bookshop, 1975 (reprint of 1899 edition).

Other Sources

"The Atlanta Campaign." *The Atlanta Historical Journal,* fall 1984.

Bierce, Ambrose, "George Thurston." *The Complete Short Stories of Ambrose Bierce.* Comp. by Ernest Jerome Hopkins. Garden City, N.Y.: Doubleday, 1970.

Brackett, Albert G., "Battle of Ezra Church." *National Tribune,* October 28, 1886.

Bragg, William Harris, "The Union General Lost in Georgia." *Civil War Times Illustrated,* June 1985.

Brown, D. Alexander, "The Battle of Brice's Cross Roads." *Civil War Times Illustrated,* April 1968.

Castel, Albert, "The Fort Pillow Massacre: A Fresh Examination of the Evidence." *Civil War History,* March 1958.

Castel, Albert, ed., "The War Album of Henry Dwight, Part I." *Civil War Times Illustrated,* February 1980.

Clauss, Errol MacGregor, "The Atlanta Campaign: 18 July — 2 September 1864." Dissertation. Emory University, 1965.

Engomar, Joseph, "Peach Tree Creek." *National Tribune,* May 10, 1883.

Hassler, William W., "A Sunny Temper and a Warm Heart." *Civil War Times Illustrated,* November 1967.

Hindman, Biscoe, "Thomas Carmichael Hindman." *Confederate Veteran,* March 1930.

Keller, Allan, "On the Road to Atlanta: Johnston vs. Sherman." *Civil War Times Illustrated,* December 1962.

McMurry, Richard Manning:
"The Atlanta Campaign: December 23, 1863 to July 18, 1864." Dissertation. Emory University, 1967.
"The Atlanta Campaign of 1864: A New Look." *Civil War History,* March 1976.
"The Hell Hole." *Civil War Times Illustrated,* February 1973.
"Kennesaw Mountain." *Civil War Times Illustrated,* January 1970.
"Resaca, 'A Heap of Hard Fiten.' " *Civil War Times Illustrated,* November 1970.

Minot, W.H.H., "At Resaca." *National Tribune,* December 16, 1886.

Osborne, Seward R., Jr., "George Young: Forgotten Hero of Peach Tree Creek." *North South Trader,* March-April 1980.

"Re-Union of Col. Dan McCook's Third Brigade, Second Division, Fourteenth A. C., August 27-29." Program. Chicago: Headquarters Third Brigade, Second Division, 14 A. C., 1900.

Ritter, William L., "Sketch of Third Battery of Maryland Artillery." *Southern Historical Society Papers,* Vol. 11.

"Special Atlanta Campaign Edition." *Civil War Times Illustrated,* July 1964.

U.S. Congressional Joint Committee on the Conduct of the War, "Fort Pillow Massacre." *Congressional Record,* GPO, May 1864.

PICTURE CREDITS

Credits from left to right are separated by semicolons, from top to bottom by dashes.

Cover: Painting by Thure de Thulstrup, courtesy Seventh Regiment Fund, Inc., photographed by Al Freni. 2, 3: Map by Peter McGinn. 8, 9: Special Collections (Orlando Poe Collection), West Point Library, U.S. Military Academy, copied by Henry Groskinsky. 10-19: Library of Congress. 21: L. M. Strayer Collection, photographed by Brian Blauser. 22, 23: Courtesy William C. Davis; Michigan State University Archives and Historical Collections; National Portrait Gallery, Smithsonian Institution, Washington, D.C., Meserve Collection No. 1369. 25: Courtesy Frank & Marie-T. Wood Print Collections, Alexandria, Va. 26: Kean Archives, Philadelphia. 28, 29: Massachusetts Commandery of the Military Order of the Loyal Legion of the United States and the U.S. Army Military History Institute (MASS/MOLLUS/USAMHI), copied by Robert Walch. 30: Painting by J. R. Walker, courtesy Confederate Memorial Association, Washington, D.C., photographed by Larry Sherer. 33: From *The Photographic History of the Civil War,* Vol. 2, edited by Francis Trevelyan Miller, published by The Review of Reviews Co., New York, 1912. 34: Library of Congress; courtesy Michael J. Winey. 36, 37: Drawings by Alfred R. Waud, Library of Congress. 39: From *The Mountain Campaigns in Georgia,* by Joseph M. Brown, published by Matthews, Northrup & Co., Buffalo, N.Y., 1890. 40: Courtesy Ted Yeatman. 41: Map by Walter W. Roberts. 42: L. M. Strayer Collection, copied by Brian Blauser. 43: Alabama Department of Archives & History — courtesy Frank & Marie-T. Wood Print Collections, Alexandria, Va. 44: From *The Mountain Campaigns in Georgia,* by Joseph M. Brown, published by Matthews, Northrup & Co., Buffalo, N.Y., 1890. 45: Courtesy Herb Peck Jr. 47: Courtesy Frank & Marie-T. Wood Print Collections, Alexandria, Va. 49: Painting by A. O. Revenough, Tennessee State Museum, photographed by Bill LaFevor. 50, 51: Sketch by J.F.E. Hillen, The New-York Historical Society. 53: Library of Congress. 55: L. M. Strayer Collection, copied by Brian Blauser. 57: Lawrence T. Jones Collection. 58, 59: Courtesy Frank & Marie-T. Wood Print Collections, Alexandria, Va.; C. Paul Loane, copied by Arthur Soll. 61: Confederate Memorial Hall, New Orleans, photographed by Bill van Calsem. 63, 65: Drawings by Alfred R. Waud, Library of Congress. 67: Map by Walter W. Roberts. 68, 69: Painting by Thure de Thulstrup, courtesy Seventh Regiment Fund, Inc., photographed by Al Freni. 70: From *The Mountain Campaigns in Georgia,* by Joseph M. Brown, published by Matthews, Northrup & Co., Buffalo, N.Y., 1890. 73: Courtesy Herb Peck Jr.; Museum of the Confederacy, Richmond — from *The Mountain Campaigns in Georgia,* by Joseph M. Brown, published by Matthews, Northrup & Co., Buffalo, N.Y., 1890. 75: L. M. Strayer Collection, copied by Brian Blauser (2); from "Re-Union of Col. Dan McCook's Third Brigade, Second Division, Fourteenth A. C., August 27-29," published by Headquarters Third Brigade, Second Division, 14 A. C., Chicago, 1900. 77: L. M. Strayer Collection, copied by Brian Blauser. 78, 79: Courtesy Betty Foster Strauss, copied and photographed by Dick Stevens. 80: MASS/MOLLUS/USAMHI, copied by A. Pierce Bounds. 81: Courtesy Frank & Marie-T. Wood Print Collections, Alexandria, Va. 82-87: The Atlanta Cyclorama, City of Atlanta, photographed by Henry Groskinsky. 88: Atlanta Historical Society; Milwaukee County Historical Society. 89: The Atlanta Cyclorama, City of Atlanta, photographed by Henry Groskinsky. 91: The J. Howard Wert Gettysburg Collection and Civil War Antiquities, photographed by Larry Sherer. 93: Courtesy Mark Katz, Americana Image Gallery. 94: Drawing by Theodore R. Davis, American Heritage Picture Collection. 96: Courtesy Seward R. Osborne, copied and photographed by Henry Groskinsky. 98: James F. Elliott Collection/USAMHI, copied by Robert Walch. 101: Map by Walter W. Roberts. 103: From *Battles and Leaders of the Civil War,* Vol. 4, published by The Century Company, New York, 1887 — painting by James E. Taylor, courtesy Atlanta Historical Society. 104: MASS/MOLLUS/USAMHI, copied by Robert Walch. 105: L. M. Strayer Collection, copied by Brian Blauser. 106: From *History of the Doles-Cook Brigade,* by Henry W. Thomas, published by Franklin Printing, Atlanta, 1903. 107: Drawing by Alfred R. Waud, Library of Congress. 108: L. M. Strayer Collection, copied by Brian Blauser. 109: Map by Walter W. Roberts. 110: From *The Mountain Campaigns in Georgia,* by

Joseph M. Brown, published by Matthews, Northrup & Co., Buffalo, N.Y., 1890. 112, 113: Courtesy Ohio Historical Society, Columbus, photographed by David R. Barker (2); Illinois State Historical Library. 114, 115: National Archives Neg. No. B-4740. 115-131: Special Collections (Orlando Poe Collection), West Point Library, U.S. Military Academy, copied by Henry Groskinsky. 133: Old State House, Arkansas Commemorative Commission. 134: Courtesy Frank & Marie-T. Wood Print Collections, Alexandria, Va. 135: Map by William L. Hezlep. 137: Iowa State Historical Department, State Historical Society; courtesy Charles E. Ennis, Lyons, N.Y. 139: National Archives Neg. No. 111-B-1561. 140: Special Collections Department, University of Georgia Libraries, Athens. 141: Rochester Museum & Science Center, Rochester, N.Y. 142: Courtesy Frank & Marie-T. Wood Print Collections, Alexandria, Va. 145: L. M. Strayer Collections, copied by Brian Blauser. 146, 147: Special Collections (Orlando Poe Collections), West Point Library, U.S. Military Academy, copied by Henry Groskinsky. 148: Museum of the Confederacy, Richmond, photographed by Larry Sherer; courtesy Bill Turner. 149: L. M. Strayer Collection, copied by Brian Blauser. 150: Drawing by Henry Otis Dwight, courtesy Ohio Historical Society, Columbus, photographed by David R. Barker. 151: Map by Walter W. Roberts. 152: MASS/MOLLUS/USAMHI, copied by Robert Walch. 153: Courtesy Frank & Marie-T. Wood Print Collection, Alexandria, Va. 154-157: Special Collections (Orlando Poe Collection), West Point Library, U.S. Military Academy, copied by Henry Groskinsky. 158, 159: Courtesy Michael J. Hammerson, London; Library of Congress. 160-165: Library of Congress. 166, 167: National Archives Neg. No. 165-SC-46. 168: Library of Congress. 169: Michigan State University Archives and Historical Collections. 170, 171: Library of Congress.

INDEX

Numerals in italics indicate an illustration of the subject mentioned.